integrating

kanban with

MRPII

automating a pull system for
enhanced JIT inventory management

integrating

kanban with

MRPII

Raymond S. Louis

PRODUCTIVITY PRESS
PORTLAND, OREGON

Additional copies of this book are available from the publisher. Discounts are available for multiple copies through the Sales Department (800-394-6868). Address all other inquiries to:

Productivity Press
P.O. Box 13390
Portland, OR 97213-0390
United States of America
Telephone: (503) 235-0600
Telefax: (503) 235-0909
E-mail: info@productivityinc.com

Cover and text design by Bill Stanton
Page composition by The Marathon Group, Inc., Durham, North Carolina
Printed and bound by BookCrafters in the United States of America

Library of Congress Cataloging-in-Publication Data

Louis, Raymond S.
    Integrating Kanban with MRPII : automating a pull system for enhanced JIT inventory management / Raymond S. Louis.
        p.   cm.
    Includes index.
    ISBN 1-56327-182-6 (hc)
        1. Inventory control—Automation.   2. Just-in-time systems.
    3. Manufacturing resource planning.   I. Title.
    TS1600.L7   1997
    658.5'1—dc21   97-28312
                                                               CIP

05 04 03 02 01   8 7 6 5 4

I DEDICATE THIS BOOK

TO THOSE WITH THE COURAGE

TO MAKE A DIFFERENCE

table of contents

publisher's message

No one needs to tell a manufacturer the importance of having the ability to obtain needed parts—when they are needed and in the amount they are needed—when building a product. And no one needs to tell a manufacturer how costly it is to run short of parts or, in an effort to compensate for shifts in customer demand, to maintain high inventories. Those who are creating a world-class manufacturing company that is responsive to the customer know that an efficient, reliable replenishment system is paramount. It does little good to reduce manufacturing processes to minutes if it still takes days to schedule its build and weeks to obtain material from the supplier.

Today there are two prevalent replenishment systems on the market that attempt to give companies some level of control over their replenishment systems: the Manufacturing Resource Planning II system (MRPII) and manual kanban. For anyone using these systems, their shortcomings are well known. While MRPII is an excellent tool in providing forward planning and integrating the relevant data of a whole organization, its push methodology fails to respond to changes in customer demand. Shifts in the master schedule require realigning and cancelling hundreds of open purchase and manufacturing orders to launch new orders. On the other hand, while the pull methodology of the manual kanban is highly responsive to customer demand (triggering replenishment as consumption occurs), whenever you plan on projected shifts in demand you need to recalculate by hand every part number to determine new kanban lot sizes or flexible work-cell staffing levels. This becomes an overwhelming task, especially when you are dealing with hundreds or thousands of kanban cards—cards you can easily lose or misplace.

In *Integrating Kanban and MRPII: Automating a Pull System for Enhanced JIT Inventory Management*, Raymond Louis provides a solution to the inherent weaknesses of these two replenishment methods. It is automated kanban or, as referred to in this book, the Automated Flow Technology™ (AFT). As Louis states, "The AFT system begins where just-in-time and manual kanban leave off." AFT is a computerized system that interfaces and integrates with the existing MRPII system to encompass manufacturing, purchasing, and the supplier base. It integrates manual kanban, bar codes, and a simplified version of electronic data interchange (EDI) to bring suppliers into the automated loop. The AFT program is inexpensive and easy to set up. Depending upon how far a company goes in developing lean production (word-class manufacturing), AFT reduces inventories, responds to shifts in customer demand, eliminates non-value-added activities in the manufacturing process, and creates a happier work force—a work force that no longer has to scramble to make production demands using an inefficient, nonresponsive replenishment system.

In Chapter 1 Louis provides an overview of the replenishment systems, including order point, and outlines the power of the automated kanban system and the ways in which AFT eliminates non-value-adding activities. Chapter 2 covers replenishment methods and provides scenarios (formulas) for calculating the different types of kanban cards for nonflexible and flexible work cells. Chapter 3 provides guidelines to develop and write your own AFT program using two separate in-house calculation programs. In Chapter 4 Louis looks at the world-class manufacturing techniques needed for a company to become a world class manufacturer (WCM). These same WCM techniques are the kanban prerequisites needed if you are to receive the full benefit of kanban. Having discussed the prerequisites for kanban the manufacturer is now ready to implement kanban. Chapter 5 discusses the basic guidelines a company needs to implement kanban for both the OEM's internal operation and the supplier base.

In Chapter 6 we come to the heart of this book: integrating Kanban and MRPII. In this chapter Louis covers step by step the key AFT computer fields (some 31 fields) and their functions, as well as the key files required to operate the AFT system. In Chapter 7 Louis provides the AFT calculations for kanban lot sizes and staffing levels. Here he discusses in depth the horizon scan and kanban calculation/simulation program (KCSP). Readers might want to take a peek a Figure 7-1 which shows you at a glance how KCSP works with MRPII. Chapter 8 explains how to perpetuate the automated kanban system using a number of reports and computer screens such as gross requirements and net requirement reports, supplier kanban trigger report, purchasing and manufacturing shortage reports, flexible work-cell staffing report, and manufacturing queue screen.

In Chapter 9 Louis covers the key topics that will help you sustain your automated kanban system, such as managing your transportation costs, mistake-proofing the triggering capability, dealing with non-work-cell kanban items, dealing with nonlinear customer demand, determining what the frequency of the kanban recalculation should be, etc. In Chapter 10 Louis presents the implementation of AFT at three fictional companies, covering their product and component profiles, their manufacturing methodologies, actions taken to implement automated kanban, and the results of full kanban implementation. These examples reflect the author's broad experience in helping companies successfully use AFT. AFT can help you reduce shortages by 80%, slash the typical order/receipt/inspect/issue response time 85%, and construct a supplier contract that will support kanban and quick changeover, reduce forms, computer transactions, phone bills, and mailing costs.

We are pleased to present to the reader the expertise of one of Productivity's consultants. Raymond Louis is the Director of Consulting for Productivity Consulting Group (PCG), a division of Productivity, Inc. He assesses facilities, develops implementation milestone charts, manages Productivity's resources in the conversion effort, and provides hands-on guidance on the shop floor with client personnel. Louis has worked in a variety of positions at prominent firms and owned his own consulting firm—giving him extensive experience in transforming traditional manufacturing operations into WCM environments. With this book, Productivity Press continues to serve its readers with the technical tools and processes needed to successfully implement the powerful methods of lean production. We know this book will help you in attaining that goal. The reader is invited to continue his or her in-house training and learning about automated kanban and other WCM techniques, using the experience of Productivity's Consulting Group (PCG).

We wish to thank all those who participated in developing and shaping the technical manuscript: Diane Asay, editor in chief; Jessica Letteney, prepress manager; Gary Peurasaari, developmental editor; Suzanne Cophenhagen copyeditor, Marianne L'Abbate proofreader; Mary Junewick production editor; The Marathon Group, Inc., compositors; and Bill Stanton, cover and text designer.

Steven Ott

President and Publisher

preface

Many companies are eliminating non-value-added activities from their manufacturing processes through the implementation of just-in-time manufacturing techniques. The goal is to reduce overall cost while improving customer response time. Unfortunately, a number of these companies are unable to realize the full benefits of their efforts due to the non-value added activities associated with their replenishment system. Essentially every activity associated with any replenishment system is non-value-added, as it does not physically transform, convert, or change the shape of the product. These non-value-added activities seriously impact customer response time and are costly to perpetuate. Little is achieved from the standpoint of customer response if the manufacturing processes are reduced to minutes, but it takes days to schedule its build and weeks to obtain material from the supplier. In addition, tremendous cost-saving opportunities are unrealized by perpetuating an ineffective system. The target for improvement should be to eliminate or streamline each activity associated with the replenishment system. This improvement must be accomplished while retaining or developing the capability to obtain what is needed, when needed, in the amount needed. The impact on cost and time for not doing so is directly proportional to (1) the level of manual efforts designed into the perpetuation and execution of the current replenishment system, (2) the quantity of active part numbers, (3) the degree of deviation of actual demand from forecasted demand within the current planning period, and (4) the amount of change in projected demand from planning period to planning period.

The most prevalent replenishment system in use today is the Manufacturing Resource Planning II (MRPII) system. Unfortunately, its MRP
(Material Requirements Planning) push methodology (see Figure 1-2)
embraces traditional techniques of work order and purchase order execution that are not responsive to changes in demand. It is also extremely
costly to operate. A shift in the master schedule requires realigning and
cancelling hundreds of open purchase and manufacturing orders in addition to launching new orders. When actual customer demand differs
from projected demand (on a daily basis), manual expedite lists must be
put together to guide the suppliers and the shop floor as to what is really
required. MRP is a slow-execution tool, though it does emphasize forward planning and integrates data relevant to the whole organization.

Kanban is a Japanese word that means "card" or "signal." The system
of kanban originated with the Toyota production system. *Manual kanban*
is a replenishment system that is responsive to demand. It is designed to
operate the just-in-time environment. A predetermined quantity is kept
on hand predicated upon future build levels, lead time, and safety stock.
The strength of the manual kanban system is that it triggers replenishment to the source of supply as consumption occurs. In this way the production floor and supplier base react to actual consumption rather than
forecasted demand. In the right environment, the manual kanban system
lowers inventory and minimizes shortages. Unfortunately, standing
alone, manual kanban has numerous shortcomings. At the heart of the
problem are the non-value-added activities of manually perpetuating
and executing it. For instance, whenever you plan on projected shifts in
demand you need to recalculate by hand every part number to determine
new kanban lot sizes or flexible work-cell staffing levels. On a daily
basis, you need to trigger replenishment by calling and/or faxing each
supplier. To respond manually to and deal with hundreds or thousands of
part numbers is cumbersome and costly. The only time you can effi-
ciently and effectively operate manual kanban is when you have only a
handful of part numbers or an exceptionally smooth demand pattern
from planning period to planning period.

There is an alternative, more powerful method than the pure application of MRP or manual kanban. It is a fully automated kanban system that integrates MRPII, kanban, bar codes, and a simplistic version of electronic data interchange (EDI). This system is also referred to in this book as the Automated Flow Technology™ (AFT). By automatically recalculating kanban lot sizes via MRP's forward projection and by triggering replenishment predicated upon consumption (demand), the AFT system can substantially lower inventory levels while significantly eliminating the non-value-added activities associated with pure MRP and manual kanban. The automated kanban system also integrates the suppliers into the automated loop with a simplistic version of electronic data interchange—optionally using bar codes to further enhance the speed and accuracy of the receipt process. It is also flexible in dealing with the issues of supplier distance and internal and external lot sizing.

By blending the forward projection capability of MRP with manual kanban pull methodology (see Figure 1-2) the AFT system significantly enhances the flexibility and competitive position of the operation. It also widens the application of kanban to environments that may not possess an exceptionally smooth demand pattern. The automated kanban system uses the forward projection capability of MRP to (1) automatically recalculate the kanban lot size, (2) perform a simulation to protect against nonlinear demand patterns, (3) inform the production areas and suppliers of the anticipated demand levels for resource planning, and (4) calculate staffing requirements for flexible work cells. The AFT system uses the information in MRPII's database to perform the calculations. Once computed, it then places the calculated kanban lot sizes and staffing requirements back into MRPII's database to await execution, at which point consumption triggers replenishment, and computer CRTs and reports reflect the required staffing levels.

The automated kanban system described in this book employs a simplified version of electronic data interchange (EDI) to download triggered orders and projected demand to the supplier base. The supplier interface is further enhanced by yearly contracts solidifying price and supplier response time. This eliminates the constant phone calls and the generation of unnecessary paper work. The elimination of these and other non-value-adding activities can significantly improve the speed, flexibility, and competitive position of most companies beyond a pure MRP or stand-alone manual kanban system.

Further, this book will help you to evaluate the manufacturing environment and individual part numbers that may not be suited for kanban. At the heart of this assessment is the evaluation of demand patterns. Kanban assumes a linear demand. If a front load or spike demand occurs, a shortage can result. The automated kanban system offers a degree of protection against nonlinear demand patterns by adjusting the kanban lot size accordingly through calculation and simulation. However, the more erratic the demand pattern, the higher inventory must be to compensate. The book also covers the method of assessment to determine at which thresholds the component may be better served on MRP than kanban. In addition, this book shows how the automated kanban system can procure selected components in the traditional MRP manner while placing the balance of the items on kanban. This is an important option, since not all components are candidates for kanban and implementing kanban is a gradual process.

As with any system, preparatory work is required. For example, to eliminate the non-value-added function of a stockroom, you should construct work cells with material located at the point of use with back-flushing capability (see Chapter 4). Container options and transportation methodologies must be selected and supplier contracts solidified. Kanban lot sizes and work-cell staffing are automatically calculated by the AFT system. All you have to do is develop simple, inexpensive in-house programming to integrate your current MRPII system with kanban. This book gives you the means to do just that.

Whether you are in a highly advanced or a start-up, just-in-time manufacturing environment, this book shows you how to automate, implement, and perpetuate an advanced automated replenishment system. You will learn how to eliminate non-value-added activities from your manufacturing processes. You will also have access to just-in-time manufacturing techniques and in-house programming to automate kanban that will further enhance your operation by reducing overall cost and improving customer response time. Once you adopt the methods of reducing non-value-added activities described in this book and program your MRPII system to run an automated kanban system, your replenishment system will, for the first time, obtain what is needed, when needed, and in the amount needed. Only then can you say that you are responding to your customers competitively.

acknowledgments

To my wife, Laurie: Thank you for reviewing the entire book to ensure that I communicated clearly. Thanks are also due my colleagues Richard Niedermeier, Charles Louis, and Richard Tech, who reviewed key portions of the text, offering their insights and recommendations. Their input was valuable and appreciated. I am grateful to Steven Ott and Diane Asay of Productivity Press, who accepted this work, and Gary Peurasaari, editor, who developed its content and enhanced its presentation. I also want to thank Suzanne Copenhagen, copyeditor, and Mary Junewick, production editor, for their attention to the detail of the presentation. Finally, I express my warm appreciation to Robert Gelber, who allowed his facility to be one of the first to fully automate the kanban process.

1

eliminating replenishment
system waste

Many companies are investing time and effort in transforming their manufacturing processes to world-class levels by deploying world-class manufacturing techniques. A number of them have achieved responsive manufacturing process capabilities, literally reducing their manufacturing process lead times from weeks to a matter of hours. These companies have moved from large batch-builds with long setups to a one-piece flow in which work cells and quick change-over are used. By deploying total productive maintenance (TPM), their equipment has become more reliable and the manufacturing environment is visually organized, displayed, and controlled through the concept of visual workplace. These techniques, in combination with total quality management (TQM), enable the manufacturing processes to be highly responsive and to produce quality at the source. Unfortunately, these process improvements alone will not create a responsive, cost-competitive manufacturer.

What companies often do not realize when implementing these manufacturing processes is the need to develop an equally responsive replenishment system. This additional requirement becomes evident to manufacturers when their replenishment system is unable to respond as rapidly to customer demand as the manufacturing processes. The net impact is often that the gains achieved from the manufacturing process conversion are compromised by an ineffective, nonresponsive replenish-ment system.

A company's conversion of its manufacturing processes to world-class levels significantly reduces cost by eliminating non-value-added activities (waste). But what about the costs of perpetuating and executing an ineffective replenishment-system methodology? Does your system rely upon antiquated execution and production-support mechanisms that are further aggravated by inaccurate forecasts? Does it require a cadre of support personnel to review reports and to create work orders, purchase orders, and other paperwork? Do you still have a stockroom? Is it filled with inventory even while shortages exist? If so, your replenishment system is awash in non-value-added activities, thus driving up the cost of your products and creating a weak link in your competitive advantage. In the end, a manufacturer's overall competitive strength is at best equal to its weakest point.

REPLENISHMENT SYSTEM REVIEW— NON-VALUE-ADDED ACTIVITIES

For manufacturers to respond rapidly and effectively to customer de-mand at the lowest possible cost, the manufacturing processes and the replenishment system must eliminate, or streamline, the non-value-added activities (see Figure 1-1). By definition, all activity associated with any replenishment system is non-value-added because it does not physically transform, convert, or change the shape of a product for cus-tomer use. The target for improvement of the replenishment system should be to eliminate or streamline each manual activity associated with it. You must accomplish this while retaining or developing the abil-ity to obtain what is needed, when needed, in the amount needed. The impact in cost and time for not doing so is directly proportional to

- The level of manual efforts designed into the perpetuation and execution of the current replenishment system

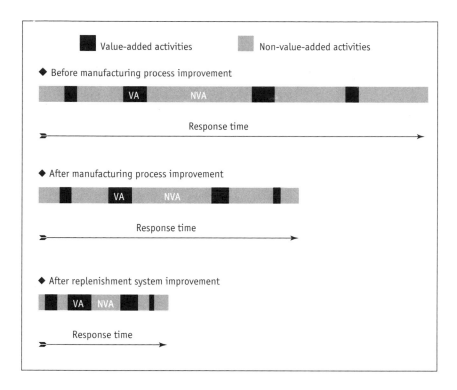

Figure 1-1. Improving Customer Response Time

- The quantity of active part numbers
- The degree of deviation of actual demand versus forecasted demand within the current planning period
- The amount of changes in projected demand from planning period to planning period

The above apply to either a push system or a pull system.

Push System Versus Pull System

There are two basic types of replenishment systems, the *push* and *pull*. The push system is associated with a fully integrated Manufacturing Resource Planning (MRPII) package that is designed to launch, realign,

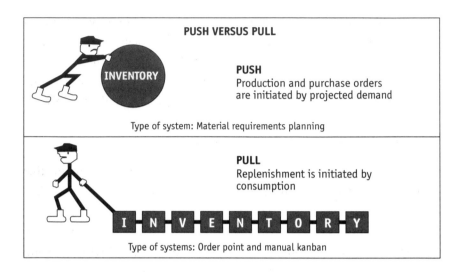

Figure 1-2. Push Versus Pull System

and cancel purchase and manufacturing orders predicated upon projected demand (see Figure 1-2). This is accomplished through the master production schedule, which encompasses customer orders and/or forecast, which in turn drive a material requirements planning (MRP) module. The MRP module determines what purchase and production orders need to be launched, realigned, or canceled to support the master production schedule. Regardless of whether consumption is taking place or not, the MRP will continue to demand that all items be procured or manufactured until a new *explosion* (computer calculation based upon a new master production schedule) is executed. This explosion will advise the user, by part number, what action to take.

The reorder point system and manual kanban system are examples of a pull system. Basically, these two pull systems employ a predetermined quantity on-hand for each part number, and consumption triggers replenishment.

All replenishment systems have different levels of waste associated with their execution and perpetuation. Every manual element adds to the response time and cost of the product. To gain an appropriate understanding of replenishment-system waste, we will discuss their most pronounced non-value-adding methodologies. In reviewing these systems, keep in mind that there are many variations to each of their applications. Chapter 2 covers the basics of these methodologies more thoroughly.

Manufacturing Resource Planning (MRPII)

MRPII employs a material requirements planning (MRP) module that launches, realigns, and cancels purchase and manufacturing orders. The basic premise of MRP is that it determines what is needed, in the amount needed, at the time needed. For example, theoretically any inventory coming in the receiving area is destined to be consumed within a short period. Unfortunately, most practitioners would agree this is far from reality, especially when incoming sales orders are different in quantity and/or mix than what was projected to occur in the master production schedule. The high levels of inventory in the stockroom and the daily shortage list bear witness to the frequency of this problem. It usually occurs as a result of inaccurate sales forecast, aggravated by long internal and external lead times. The long delays created by the manual steps of traditional MRPII methodology also prevent you from responding rapidly to shifting customer demand (see Figure 1-3). The following are non-value-added steps in traditional MRPII methodology:

Step 1. The material planning department analyzes the MRP to determine what needs to be procured. They pull buy cards for each part number and write out the specifics of what to procure. They then give the buy card to the buyer along with a computerized list of open purchase orders that need to be realigned or canceled.

Step 2. The purchasing department groups/sorts the buy cards by suppliers, phone suppliers, negotiating price, and delivery of each buy item; realigns existing purchase orders; and performs cancellations. They then give the card to the purchasing clerk, who inputs the purchase order information into the MRPII system and generates hard copy purchase

Material Planning Dept.	Purchasing Dept.	Receiving Dept.	Inspection Dept.	Stockroom	Production Control
• Analyze MRP • Pull buy cards • Specify what to procure • Generate list of open purchase orders to realign/cancel	• Group buy cards by supplier • Phone suppliers • Negotiate price and delivery • Realign/Cancel • Input P.O. • Log P.O. info on buy card • Print P.O./Burst/ Distribute/Mail/File • File buy card	• Open Pkg./Locate paperwork • View open P.O. screen • Count • Input receipt • Forward parts to Inspection Dept.	• Inspect parts • Deliver parts to stockroom	• Check for part shortages • Fill part shortages • Put away material • Pick work orders • Input quantity pulled and shortages into computer • Deliver to floor	• Analyze MRP • Create new work orders • Realign/Cancel open new work orders • Develop shortage list based upon what is really required • Expedite

Response time

Figure 1-3. MRPII Non-Value-Added Activities

orders. These purchase orders are then burst, mailed, distributed, and filed. The buy cards are then refiled.

Step 3. The receiving department opens all the incoming packages and locates supplier paperwork identifying the contents. They then pull up from the computer the purchase order number, count the parts, and key the supplier receipt into the system. Finally, they forward the parts to the inspection department.

Step 4. The inspection department checks the parts as to specification and delivers the parts to the stockroom.

Step 5. The stockroom checks for shortages, fills the shortages, and puts material away. They then pick work orders, input the quantity and any shortages into the computer, and then deliver the work orders to the production floor.

Step 6. The production control department analyzes the MRP to determine what new work orders need to be created. They create new work orders, realign and cancel existing work orders, and develop and expedite shortage lists based upon what is really required.

It is easy to see why such a system is not responsive to shifts in customer demand. The situation is magnified when there is a shift in projected demand in an environment that has thousands of part numbers. Companies have attempted to eliminate some of these non-value-added and costly activities by the following methods:

- Adopting the buyer/planner concept, thus eliminating buy cards.
- Locating the material at the point of use at the work cell and perform backflushing (see Chapter 4). This eliminates kitting (stockroom pulls) and its related paperwork.
- Instituting a vendor certification program that permits the suppliers' material to go directly to the floor after being received.

Certainly these are steps in the right direction but they only touch on part of the non-value-added activities. A manufacturer still needs to eliminate or streamline the following non-value-added activities to have an effective replenishment system.

- The buyer/planner analyzes each part number on the MRP report to determine what action needs to be taken.
- The buyer/planner phones each supplier and negotiates price and delivery on each part required and realigns or cancels specific components. The volume of this activity is dependent upon the degree of shift in demand and quantity of part numbers.
- The buyer/planner keys in the computer-launched purchase orders, realignments, and cancellations, and generates hard copy purchase orders that are then burst, mailed, distributed, and filed.
- The receiving department opens incoming cartons, looks for the supplier paperwork that identifies the contents, pulls the purchase order numbers from the computer, counts the parts, and enters the receipt into the computer.
- The production control department generates and expedites shortage lists based upon what is really required.

Even if you do address these issues, you will still have to deal with the long external supplier lead times. You must reduce this in order to respond to shifts in customer demand. Even if a manufacturer can determine its needs relatively quickly and has a lean internal manufacturing capability, it will still respond to customer demand ineffectively unless its suppliers react to its demands as swiftly. Another serious drawback in traditional MRPII environments is their history of competitive bidding with their suppliers, which undermines the partnership-building required to reduce supplier lead times in the newer, leaner manufacturing environments.

The foregoing discussion is not an attempt to discredit MRPII but to recognize its limitations. MRPII's inherent strengths are its ability to provide forward projection planning and its database. Chapter 3 discusses the methodologies that capitalize on these strengths in eliminating non-value-added activities.

Order Point System

The order point system has been around for many years. It was the mainstay of many manufacturers prior to the advent of MRP. The order point formula is *demand during lead time plus safety stock*. From a user's perspective, the formula translates to *average daily demand (ADD) times lead time plus safety stock.*

The order point quantity is what must be on-hand when the order point system is initiated. Once the order point is reached through consumption, a replenishment order is launched. Usually the replenishment order quantity is equal to the order point quantity with minimum and multiple considerations (see Chapter 6). However, you can base it upon an economical order quantity formula (which balances machine setup cost or ordering cost with inventory carrying cost) or according to order launching interval (for example, order every three months).

The order point and order quantity calculations are still done predominantly by hand using historical usage data. However, it is computerized from a triggering standpoint as the order point quantity is continuously compared to the total of on-hand and on-order quantities by the system. If this combined total falls below the order point, the computerized system raises a flag on the reorder point report to inform the user to launch a replenishment order.

With the exception of realignments, most of the non-value-added activities under the MRPII system apply to order point. Launched orders under the order point system are typically not realigned. However, the hand recalculation of the order point and order quantity should be added to the list of non-value-added activities. This is a major issue. It is such a time consuming process that it is rarely recalculated. Another issue is that recalculation is typically based on historical usage instead of forward projection. Finally, order point relies on linear usage (an equal quantity consumed each day), which in practice rarely occurs. Batch build is the norm in these environments. The end result is part shortages coupled with high inventory.

Order point's strength lies in its simplicity and its easily understood methods for calculating and perpetuating. Unfortunately, the need for manual recalculation, use of historical data for recalculation, and batch-build render it ineffective.

Manual Kanban

Kanban is a Japanese word that means "card" or "signal." The manual kanban system was designed to operate a lean manufacturing environment. There are three types of cards that initiate action in the manual kanban system.

1. *Production card.* Authorizes the cell responsible for replenishment to produce the item.
2. *Move card.* Authorizes the cell using the in-house make components to obtain replenishment from the cell responsible for producing replenishment.
3. *Supplier card.* Authorizes the cell using supplier components to obtain replenishment from the supplier.

There are many variations to the formula for determining the quantity of kanban cards (one per container) released into or retracted from the overall system. However, they all employ the variables of average daily demand, lead time, safety stock, and standard container capacity (standard quantity of parts in a container).

The ADD is predicated upon forward projection. You recalculate the number of move cards and supplier cards when the forward projection indicates a shift in projected demand. You must also recalculate the number of production cards for nonflexible work cells (cells that cannot add or subtract workers) or you have to adjust the production rate of a flexible work cell by adding or subtracting workers. The build is load-smooth and sequenced at the top level to provide a smooth usage of all lower level assemblies and components throughout the facility. This is required because kanban, like order point, requires a linear usage. Like MRPII and order point, non-value-added activities in the manual kanban system hinder a rapid response to shifts in customer demand (see Figure 1-4). Specifically:

- Each time there is a shift in projected demand, each purchase part and nonflexible work cell part number must have its *kanban lot size* recalculated by hand. This is the same problem encountered with order point. Also, like order point, recalculation probably will not take place in environments that have hundreds or thousands of part numbers. End result—high inventory coupled with shortages.
- Each time a purchased kanban is triggered, someone must phone or fax the triggered order to the supplier. The problem usually occurs when the supplier does not receive the signal. At this point, the work cell might find out that the signal for an order was not sent, or someone at the supplier's central fax machine picked it up by accident. End result—a shortage.
- The suppliers and internal manufacturing areas need to plan their capacity levels for future demand. A manual kanban system does not have a projected demand report by part number that reflects hours. How can you prepare for future demand levels without the visibility of or access to expected demand that the MRPII system gives you? Even if you manually prepare a projected demand report, it will take many, many hours to complete. By that time precious response time will have been lost.
- When an internal assembly is triggered for replenishment, all the components may not be available. There is no easy way in a manual kanban system to know whether all the parts are

---

Minimum Impact

- Kanban lot sizes recalculated manually (long response time to shifts in demand).
- Suppliers phoned/faxed (long response time).
- Kanban cards physically collected (lost).
- No planning capability for capacity planning (understaffed/over staffed).
- No parts simulation capability prior to build (partially made items waiting for shortage).
- Kanban cards end up on floor.
- Difficult to ascertain the current load at each cell to shift personnel.

Typical Impact

- Kanban lot sizes are not recalculated (stock out).
- Simulations looking for front loads and spike demands do not occur (stock out).
- Kanban cards are not picked up on time (stock out).
- Supplier never received the fax (stock out).

Figure 1-4. Impact of Manual Kanban Non-Value-Added Activites

available prior to starting the build. End result—partially made product waiting for the short components.

- The manufacturing triggering device, be it a poker chip or card for manufactured items, often ends up on the shop floor. End result—a shortage.
- Current load information that expresses hours by individual work cell and reflects what has been triggered is not easy to obtain. End result—without this data it is difficult to determine what operators to shift from work cell to work cell.

AUTOMATED KANBAN SYSTEM—WASTE ELIMINATION

Once you understand the drawbacks of a manual kanban system, you will appreciate how a properly designed and implemented automated kanban system, a system that is integrated with MRPII, substantially eliminates waste. An automated kanban system will improve the following areas:

- It will automatically recalculate all the identified kanban part numbers each time MRP is generated. Included in this process are a routine for calculating kanban that adjusts for front loads and spike demands and a simulation model that tests the newly recalculated kanban lot size against projected demand for potential stock-outs.

- It will download a one-line, per part number, projected demand to the supplier each time MRP is run. This is performed on a simplified version of electronic data interchange (EDI), which only takes a few hours to set up each supplier. The supplier uses this projected demand for capacity planning only (only consumption triggers replenishment).

- It will automatically create and download a purchase order to the supplier when a supplier kanban item is triggered by consumption. All the detail for the creation of the order is housed in the MRPII's database.

- It will automatically generate staffing requirements for work cells based upon the average daily demand, labor content per unit, and operator effective time per day.

- It will display triggered internal kanban items at the computer terminal located in the cell responsible for replenishment. Prior to authorizing a release to build, a parts-availability simulation will take place to ensure that all the components are available. If all the parts are available, a bar-coded manufacturing traveler is summoned to print out when the operator is ready to run the item. You can also use the bar-coded manufacturing traveler to initiate machines, perform deduct point/backflush activity, and a number of other functions. If all the parts are not available, an exception report is generated that shows what is missing and when it is due.

- It will automatically indicate the current manufacturing load of *triggered* kanbans expressed in hours at the computer terminal of each cell.

- It will utilize optional methods to further reduce non-value-added activities. For example, incoming bar-coded kanban containers are placed on a modified electronic scale and scanned. This automatically brings up the purchase order, determines the quantity in the container, and performs the receipt if the count is in compliance.

The automated kanban system significantly reduces the non-value-added activities associated with MRPII, order point, or manual kanban. By combining the strengths of MRPII, manual kanban, bar codes, and a simplified version of EDI, automated kanban creates an extremely powerful pull system that enhances the manufacturer's overall flexibility—significantly reducing both time and cost in responding to customer demand. Only when a company develops a highly responsive replenishment system will it reap the full benefits of transforming its manufacturing processes to world-class levels.

In Chapter 2, we further discuss replenishment system basics of MRPII, order point, and manual kanban, focusing on the manual kanban card calculation and the classical rules for its application. If you are already well versed in these basics, you can move on to Chapter 3 for an overview of the automated kanban system.

2

replenishment system basics

Understanding order point, material requirements planning, and manual kanban takes many hours of study. It is necessary, however, since there is no escaping the need to understand them. Those who are on MRP preparing for kanban will discover that not all part numbers are kanban candidates. In most cases, this requires the continuation of MRP even if a manual kanban system is being considered. An understanding of order point is also essential so as not to repeat the same errors with kanban. Order point is very closely related to kanban. As noted in Chapter 1, problems with order point are due largely to infrequent recalculation and the use of historical usage versus forward projection. There is never enough time to recalculate order points manually. With manual kanban, too, the kanban lot size must be recalculated when demand is projected to shift.

Recalculation must be done in a way that eliminates the non-value-added activities that impact both the cost and response time to customer needs; therefore, the successful application of any replenishment system requires a thorough knowledge of the basics. This is especially true when designing and implementing an automated kanban system, since it is an outgrowth of existing methodologies. This chapter provides a basic foundation for understanding automated kanban by presenting an overview of MRPII, order point, and the manual kanban system. It then focuses on the manual kanban card calculation and classical rules for application.

MRPII OVERVIEW

The MRPII is a fully integrated, closed-loop system. It is integrated because it shares a common database servicing the whole organization, and it is closed-loop because production information is updated into the replenishment system for replanning. The MRPII system is used in make-to-order, repetitive, and job-shop environments. It is a push system that is considered the mainstay of North American replenishment systems. A push system requests items to be produced and/or procured to support the master production schedule. Regardless of whether the master production schedule is in keeping with actual incoming customer orders, it continues on its planned course until there is a new master production schedule followed by an MRP *explosion* (the calculation process of the MRP module) recommending new action.

A number of modules make up the MRPII system. Each module plays a specific role in the planning and execution of requirements. We concentrate on the following ones:

- Master production schedule module
- Material requirements planning module
- Shop scheduling module
- Capacity requirements planning module

Master Production Schedule Module

The master production schedule module drives the material requirements planning module. The master production schedule encompasses customer orders as well as the forecasted demand of final product (see Table 2-1). The master production schedule reflects the final product part number, quantity, and time period. In each planning period the materials department should jointly develop the master production schedule with the

Table 2.1. Master Production Schedule "Product A"

Day	1	2	3	4	5	6	7	8	9	10	11	12
Customer orders	3	2	0	0	0	0	0	0	0	0	0	0
Forecast	7	8	10	10	12	15	15	15	15	15	15	15
Total	10	10	10	10	12	15	15	15	15	15	15	15

sales and manufacturing departments. During the master production schedule's construction, it is best to use rough capacity estimates for the plant's key resource centers so as not to make an unrealistic demand on the shop. In addition, some applications of the master production schedule use *time fences* that define and restrict the degree of allowable changes within a specific period. Usually these changes are not permitted within the lead time that it takes to acquire material and manufacture the product (*critical path*). This means that the master production schedule is frozen in the beginning time periods, thus relieving the operation/supplier base from having to react to shifts in customer demand within a defined frozen period.

Material Requirements Planning Module

The material requirements planning (MRP) module is a computerized calculation tool that supports the master production schedule by determining the quantity required and respective due dates and release dates of new purchase and manufacturing orders. It also recommends the realignment and cancellation of existing orders. The calculation process of the MRP module, known as an *explosion*, begins with the master production schedule and continues level by level down the bill of materials until it hits the lowest level component or raw material (see Figure 2-1). This explosion process uses the bill of materials, quantity on hand, open purchase and manufacturing orders, and lead time to determine the quantity required and the respective release date.

The MRP module has the capability to lot-size the net-offset requirements (planned order release) according to the order policy code. You

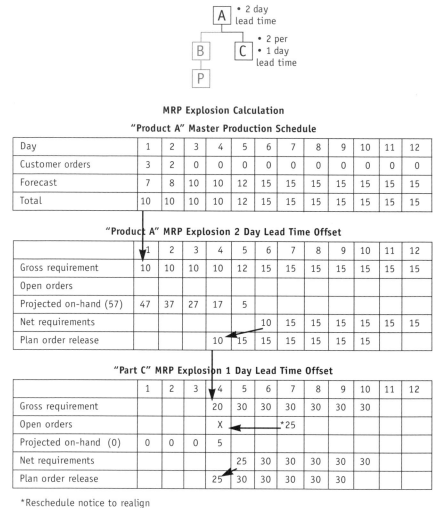

Bill of Material

MRP Explosion Calculation

"Product A" Master Production Schedule

Day	1	2	3	4	5	6	7	8	9	10	11	12
Customer orders	3	2	0	0	0	0	0	0	0	0	0	0
Forecast	7	8	10	10	12	15	15	15	15	15	15	15
Total	10	10	10	10	12	15	15	15	15	15	15	15

"Product A" MRP Explosion 2 Day Lead Time Offset

	1	2	3	4	5	6	7	8	9	10	11	12
Gross requirement	10	10	10	10	12	15	15	15	15	15	15	15
Open orders												
Projected on-hand (57)	47	37	27	17	5							
Net requirements							10	15	15	15	15	15	15
Plan order release					10	15	15	15	15	15	15		

"Part C" MRP Explosion 1 Day Lead Time Offset

	1	2	3	4	5	6	7	8	9	10	11	12
Gross requirement				20	30	30	30	30	30	30		
Open orders				X			*25					
Projected on-hand (0)	0	0	0	5								
Net requirements					25	30	30	30	30	30		
Plan order release				25	30	30	30	30	30			

*Reschedule notice to realign

Figure 2-1. MRP Explosion

can set the order policy code for *discrete* (one-for-one) or use any number of other lot-sizing options that group the netted discrete requirements according to the setting.

Shop Scheduling Module

The shop scheduling module uses open work orders and planned work order due dates from MRP's explosion to calculate individual start dates and completion dates for each operation of each part number. One of the outputs is a dispatch report by work center (see Figure 2-2). This in turn is used as a production schedule for the shop floor.

Capacity Requirements Planning Module

The capacity requirements planning module uses the information from the shop scheduling module to determine the projected load expressed in hours by work center and date (see Figure 2-3). You use this module to plan sufficient resources to meet the master production schedule.

Work Center 453			**Dispatch Report**				11/10/97
Part number	Description	Quantity	Work order number	Start date	Due date	Setup hours	Run hours
135-67	Spindle	650	3223	11/10/97	11/11/97	1.50	8.50
124-45	Bearing	750	3554	11/11/97	11/12/97	1.12	9.00
176-92	Sleeve	925	2582	11/12/97	11/14/97	1.50	11.00
				Total hours		4.12	28.50

Figure 2-2. Dispatch Report

	Capacity Load Report 11/10/97									
Work Center		11/14	11/21	11/28	12/5	12/12	12/19	12/26	1/2	1/9
453	Capacity	38.3	38.3	38.3	38.3	38.3	38.3	38.3	38.3	38.3
	load	32.6	36.0	42.0	45.0	48.8	55.8	49.3	45.5	38.7
	+/−	+5.7	+2.3	−3.7	−6.7	−10.5	−17.5	−11.0	−7.2	−0.4
555	Capacity									

Figure 2-3. Capacity Load Report

ORDER POINT SYSTEM OVERVIEW

The order point system is usually manual in its calculation, but its trig-gering for replenishment uses a computerized report, since the order point and order quantity are keyed into and monitored by the system. When the combined total of on-hand and on-order falls below the order point quantity, an order for replenishment is automatically flagged on a report. The hand-calculated order quantity is then launched. The equation for determining order point is equal to the demand during lead time plus safety stock. In application, order point uses the following formula: average daily demand (ADD) times lead time (LT) plus safety stock (SS). You usually base the ADD on the history of demand as opposed to the projected demand.

$$\text{Order point} = (\text{ADD}) \, (\text{LT} + \text{SS})$$

An example of the order point formula looks like this:

$$\text{Order point} = (150 \text{ ADD}) \times (5 \text{ day LT} + 2 \text{ day SS}) = 1{,}050$$

The order point informs the user when to launch a replenishment order to the shop or supplier. The quantity that is ordered is usually either equal to the order point quantity or in excess of it, depending upon

- Desired ordering frequency
- Setup time considerations
- Cost of the component
- Supplier minimum and multiple order quantity

The order point system requires a linear demand pattern. It is often found in repetitive manufacturing and job shops where a high degree of component commonality at the lower levels tends to smooth out the demand patterns. Order point is classified as a pull system. In a pull system, consumption triggers replenishment.

MANUAL KANBAN SYSTEM OVERVIEW

The kanban system originated in the Toyota production system (or lean manufacturing). One of the pillars supporting lean manufacturing is just-in-time (JIT). In a flow process, for example, JIT means that the right parts needed in assembly reach the assembly line at the time they are needed and only in the amount needed. Kanban is the operating method that manages and ensures JIT production. Kanban, like order point, is a pull system. It authorizes production or delivery of required items initiated by consumption and is the means by which the lean production system moves smoothly. The kanban card carries the information vertically and laterally within a company and between the company and suppliers. In the kanban system, all movements in the plant can be unified or systematized, thus synchronizing the whole shop to work together through the build of final product.

The following are several rules that must be applied to a manual kanban system. Without these manual kanban rules, the system cannot succeed.

- Only quality parts are sent to subsequent processes. Quality is ensured prior to placing the parts into the containers.
- The operators from the subsequent operations obtain their own parts.
- Nothing is made or moved without a kanban card.
- Only manufacture the specific quantity that was pulled by the subsequent process.
- The final assembly schedule must be load-smooth and sequenced.
- The production process should be standardized and stabilized.

With these kanban rules in place you can base the final product build upon a frozen production schedule or on one that is responsive to customer demand. In either case, in the kanban system the consumption of supporting assemblies and components triggers replenishment authorization in the form of internal move cards, production cards, and supplier cards (see Figure 2-4). In other applications the broadcast method is used to signal authorization to produce and deliver the required item to the point of use.

Internal Move Card

Final assembly lines and work cells designate storage spaces known as *inbound* and *outbound* areas. The inbound area contains raw material, components, and/or subassemblies in standard containers that supply the work cell or assembly line in producing its assigned items; the outbound area contains the completed items it is responsible for producing. If it is an internally produced item, each container in the inbound area has an internal move card attached (see Figure 2-5). When consumption begins on a container, the cell using the material detaches the internal move card and takes it to the cell responsible for replenishment. The work cell responsible for replenishment has completed items staged in its outbound area. The user attaches the one move card on the container being taken, and then transports both the move card and container housing the replenishment back to the inbound area of the using assembly line or work cell. The internal move card should only circulate between the using assembly line or work cell and the cell responsible for replenishment.

Production Card

The cell responsible for replenishment already has a quantity of completed items that it makes waiting in the outbound area. Each of the containers in this outbound area has a production card attached. When the final assembly or work cell brings its internal move card to obtain replenishment, it will remove the production card from the container

Internal Move Card

Part number _2347_   Description _Mach base_

Replenishment work cell no. _22_

Outbound stock location _G5_

Inbound stock location _A6_

Container capacity	Container type
200 pieces	2S

Production Card

Part number _2347_   Description _Mach base_

Replenishment work cell no. _22_

Outbound stock location _G5_

Container capacity	Container type
200 pieces	2S

Supplier Move Card

Supplier _ABC Casting Corporation_

Part number _2346_   Description _Base casting_

Container capacity _200 pieces_

Container type _2S_

Deliver to inbound location _Q7_

Figure 2-4. Kanban Cards

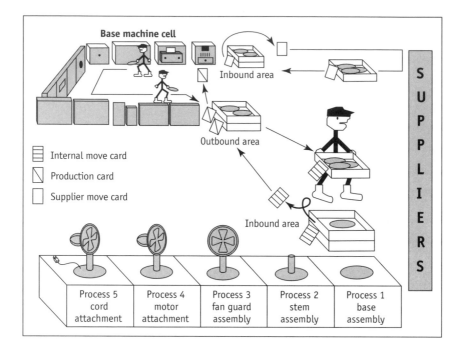

Figure 2-5. Manual Kanban Card Movement

housing the replenishment and give it to the work cell responsible for
replenishment. This authorizes the work cell responsible for replenishment to replenish what is taken. Once the replenishment cell produces
the quantity on the production card, it attaches the production card to
the appropriate size container and places it in the outbound area. The
production card is only circulated within the producing work cell and its
outbound area.

The cell responsible for replenishment consumes other internally
produced components in its replenishment efforts. These components are
located in the replenishment cell's inbound area. Internal move cards are
attached to these containers if they are internally produced, and are
detached and given to the cell responsible for its replenishment once
consumption begins.

This production card and internal move card process cascades all the way down to the lowest level component, creating a pull effect throughout the whole shop.

Supplier Card

You use the supplier card to obtain replenishment from the supplier if the part is a purchase item. The supplier card, like the internal move card, is attached to the container located at the inbound location of the final assembly line or work cell. When consumption begins on the container, the user removes the supplier card and forwards it to the supplier responsible for replenishment. The supplier will then provide the replenishment called out on the supplier card and reattach the card to the container. The container with the attached supplier card will then be delivered back to its inbound location.

Broadcast

Broadcast is a system that sends a (typically electronic) signal from the beginning of the final assembly line to the responsible work cell or supplier and authorizes production and delivery of the required item (see Figure 2-6). You do not keep broadcast items on-hand prior to notification; rather it is a method used for items that can be manufactured or procured and delivered to the point of use after notification, just prior to a need.

Load-Smoothing and Sequencing

To apply kanban properly you must have a linear, cyclical demand pattern for the quantity of final product that is built during the course of the day. This is achieved through *load-smoothing* and *sequencing* your final assembly level. Load-smoothing is a method for developing a daily build schedule that levels the peaks and valleys of the overall quantity of the final product that is to be built each day. To load-smooth the final

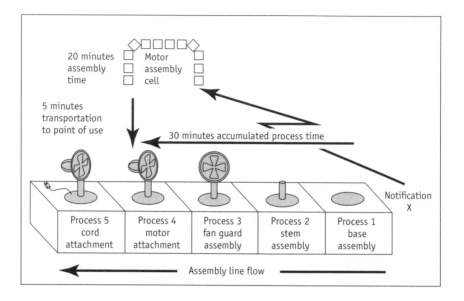

Figure 2-6. Kanban Broadcast

assembly schedule, take the monthly build quantity and divide it by the number of work days in the month. In the example shown in Table 2-2, 240 Qs, 120 Rs, and 60 Ss will be built each day. Load-smoothing is the first step in making your build quantity linear. These daily quantities are then further refined by sequencing.

Sequencing is a technique to determine the order for producing the final product throughout the day. The objective of sequencing is to create a linear, cyclical demand pattern during the course of the day. This enhances the work cells' ability to respond more effectively to shifting customer demand. The following example explains how to sequence the final build schedule.

Example for products Q, R, S.   First, determine the *takt time* for each product. The takt time is the production rate at which the product needs to be produced to achieve the daily build quantity. To determine the takt time, take the total working minutes in a day that are scheduled for pro-

Table 2-2. Load Smoothing

Final product	Month build quantity	Working days in month		Daily build quantity
Q	4800	/20	=	240
R	2400	/20	=	120
S	1200	/20	=	60

Table 2-3. Takt Time

Final product	Minutes in a work day	Daily build quantity	Takt time
Q	460 minutes	/240	1.9166 minutes
R	460 minutes	/120	3.8333 minutes
S	460 minutes	/60	7.6666 minutes

duction and divide by the required daily build quantity of each product (see Table 2-3). In this example, it is 480 minutes minus two 10 minute breaks. Also in this example, one Q needs to be built every 1.9166 minutes, one R every 3.8333 minutes, and one S every 7.6666 minutes.

Next, find the lowest common denominator that each of the product takt times will divide into equally. The lowest common denominator in this example is 7.6666 minutes. Now divide each of the individual product's takt time into the 7.6666 minutes to determine how much of each product will be built in that period of time. In this example, it is 4 Qs (7.6666/1.9166), 2 Rs (7.6666/3.8333), and 1 S (7.6666/7.6666). These quantities need to be built in a 7.6666-minute sequence cycle. Finally, lay the 4 Qs, 2 Rs, and 1 S in the most rhythmic sequence as shown below.

7.6666-minute sequence cycle
QRQSQRQ

This sequence cycle will be repeated 60 times within each work day (460 minutes per work day divided by the 7.6666 minute sequence cycle). To double check the calculation, multiply the quantity of product produced in the 7.6666 minute cycle times the number of times the sequence cycle will repeat (60), as shown in Table 2-4.

Table 2-4. Verifying Daily Build Quantity

Final product	Quantity made in 7.6666 minute cycle	Number of cycles in 460 minutes		Total made in work day
Q	(4)	(60)	=	240
R	(2)	(60)	=	120
S	(1)	(60)	=	60

This load-smooth, sequenced, final build schedule activates the kan-ban pull system when consumption begins at the final assembly level. The end result is a synchronized factory and supplier base.

MANUAL KANBAN SYSTEM—KANBAN CALCULATION

As discussed above, the three basic types of kanban cards are the pro-duction kanban card, the internal move kanban card, and the supplier kanban card. Although many formulas are used to determine the num-ber of kanban cards, there are only four basic variables in any multiple-container calculation formula, regardless of the formula you use:

1. Average daily demand (ADD)
2. Lead time (LT)
3. Safety stock (SS) (expressed as a decimal; for example, 1.05 = 5% increase)
4. Standard container capacity (SCC)

As shown in the following kanban card formula:

$$\text{Number of kanban cards} = \frac{(ADD)\ (LT)\ (1+.00\ SS)}{(SCC)}$$

The top part of the equation is referred to as the *kanban lot size*. This is the quantity that must be on hand when first initiating a kanban. It is the starting level of inventory that will continue to support production as replenishment orders are triggered and received. The bottom part of the equation is the *kanban order quantity*. It becomes the order quantity when consumption first begins on a container in the multiple-container kanban application. Other kanban container options use the top portion of the formula as the order quantity and are triggered in different ways. Each container option has its own application and is covered further in the following chapters. In later sections, we apply the kanban card formula to determine the number of cards for

- Production cards for nonflexible work cells
- Production cards for flexible work cells
- Internal move cards
- Supplier cards

Production Card Calculation for Nonflexible Work Cells

Nonflexible work cells are unable to change the *cell production rate* (output rate of the cell expressed as time per piece by part number) by adding and subtracting operators. Operators are added or subtracted in response to an increase or decrease in the average daily demand. Adding and subtracting operators maintains the lead time for flexible work cells and enables a static quantity of production cards. Nonflexible work cells cannot add or subtract operators because of the need to avoid a situation in which the operator waits for the machine rather than the machine waiting for the operator. In such cases, the cell is unable to add and subtract workers to affect the time per piece. A number of facilities can still benefit from a kanban system, however, even though the work cells are not yet flexible. Since the number of workers cannot be adjusted, the number of production cards must be recalculated each time the average daily demand changes.

Using the kanban card formula on an on-going basis for this purpose is straightforward. When setting up a kanban system, however, some practitioners have difficulty in establishing the lead time for a nonflexible work cell. The lead time is important to determine, since you will be using it for future kanban lot-size calculations. This lead time is predicated upon the highest expected demand that the cell was designed to produce. As might be expected, the lead time and the average daily demand determine the number of cards. When the average daily demand increases, so does the number of cards; but if the lead time employed on an on-going basis was based upon the lowest demand, it may stock-out when a higher demand is encountered. This is because the greater the demand, the longer the lead time; the longer the lead time, the greater the number of cards required.

In the following pages, we demonstrate the method to determine lead time for a nonflexible work cell. We then apply lead time to the kanban card formula to calculate the number of production cards for a multiple-container application for a nonflexible work cell. The lead time is then used on an on-going basis.

Determining Lead Time for a Nonflexible Work Cell

There are nine steps in determining the lead time for a nonflexible work cell.

Step 1. Determine the highest ADD that the work cell was designed to experience for all components made in the work cell. As shown in Table 2-5, work cell number 4 is responsible for producing part numbers A, B, and C. These part numbers go into building the final products Q, R, and S, products that have already been load-smoothed and sequenced. For the purpose of this example the quantities of Q, R, and S were the highest demand anticipated. The highest ADD for A = 480 pieces per day, B = 360 pieces per day, and C = 240 pieces per day.

Table 2-5. Determining the Highest ADD

Final assembly product	Highest final assembly build quantity	Components made in work cell #4	Quantity per assembly	Highest average daily demand	Container capacity
Q	240	A	2	480	20
R	120	B	3	360	15
S	60	C	4	240	10

Table 2-6. Total Extended Run Time per Day

Part number	Highest average daily demand	Cell production rate	Extended run time per day in minutes
A	480	.25	120 minutes
B	360	.30	108 minutes
C	240	.30	+ 72 minutes
			300 minutes

Step 2. Determine the *total extended run time* required for work cell number 4. The total extended run time per day totals 300 minutes for parts A, B, and C (see Table 2-6).

Step 3. Determine the total time available for production in work cell number 4 by taking the number of minutes per shift and subtracting the number of minutes for breaks. If the work cell is down for lunch, preventive maintenance, or any other considerations, deduct it from the number of minutes per shift also. In this example there is one 480-minute shift that has two 10-minute breaks.

480 minutes per day
−20 minutes breaks
460 minutes per day available for production

Step 4. Determine the *total setup time* required to produce *one sequence cycle* of parts A, B, C in the replenishment work cell. In the following example, it takes a 20-minute setup time for one sequence cycle.

Part number	Setup time
A	7 minutes
B	6 minutes
C	7 minutes
	20 minutes setup time for one sequence cycle

Step 5. Determine the available time for setup by subtracting minutes of total run time from minutes per day available for production. In this example available time for setup is 160 minutes.

460 minutes per day available

–300 minutes total run time

160 minutes available for setup

Step 6. Determine the number of times the sequence cycle can be set up for A, B, and C. In this example it is eight times.

$$\frac{160 \text{ minutes available for setup}}{20 \text{ minutes total setup time for A, B, and C}} = 8 \text{ times}$$

Step 7. Determine the *lot size* that must be produced for each part number each time it is set up.

$$\text{Part A} = \frac{480 \text{ pieces/day}}{8 \text{ setups}} = 60 \text{ piece lot size}$$

$$\text{Part B} = \frac{360 \text{ pieces/day}}{8 \text{ setups}} = 45 \text{ piece lot size}$$

$$\text{Part C} = \frac{240 \text{ pieces/day}}{8 \text{ setups}} = 30 \text{ piece lot size}$$

Step 8. Determine the *manufacturing lead time* for parts A, B, and C by using the data ascertained in the prior steps.

Part Number A: 7 min. setup time + 15.0 min. run time (60 pieces @ .25) = 22.0 minutes

Part Number B: 6 min. setup time + 13.5 min. run time (45 pieces @ .30) = 19.5 minutes

Part Number C: 7 min. setup time + 9.0 min. run time (30 pieces @ .30) = 16.0 minutes

One sequence = 57.5 minutes total MFG lead time

Although part number C requires a 7-minute setup and has a run time of 9.0 minutes for a lot size of 30 pieces, its manufacturing lead time includes the setup time and run time of part numbers A and B. You must also add any other lead-time elements to the manufacturing lead time, such as inspecting finished parts.

Step 9. Determine the manufacturing lead time in relationship to the minutes available for production in a work day by dividing the minutes per day available for production into the minutes total manufacturing lead time. Express this as a whole number or decimal. In the following example the manufacturing lead time for a day is 0.125.

$$\frac{57.5 \text{ minutes total MFG lead time}}{460 \text{ minutes per day available for production}} = 0.125 \text{ day MFG lead time}$$

Each time the ADD changes, the manufacturing lead time of 0.125 of a day will be used for part numbers A, B, and C in the kanban card formula for recalculating the number of production cards for a nonflexible work cell.

Nonflexible Work-Cell Production-Card Calculation

Once the lead time is ascertained, it is applied to the kanban formula on an on-going basis. The average daily demand will change, but the lead time will remain constant unless the conditions on which it was predicated change significantly. The lead time is applied to the kanban formula as shown below. For this example, we assume that the current average daily demand is 480 pieces for part number A, 360 pieces for part number B, and 240 pieces for part number C. The LT is 0.125, with a zero safety stock (SS). This formula is used on an on-going basis.

$$\text{Part A} = \frac{(480 \text{ pcs. ADD}) (0.125 \text{ LT}) (1 + .00 \text{ SS})}{20\text{-piece standard container capacity}} = 3 \text{ production kanban cards}$$

$$\text{Part B} = \frac{(360 \text{ pcs. ADD}) (0.125 \text{ LT}) (1 + .00 \text{ SS})}{15\text{-piece standard container capacity}} = 3 \text{ production kanban cards}$$

$$\text{Part C} = \frac{(240 \text{ pcs. ADD}) (0.125 \text{ LT}) (1 + .00 \text{ SS})}{10\text{-piece standard container capacity}} = 3 \text{ production kanban cards}$$

Most part numbers forced to batch size due to long setup times cannot react to the triggering of individual containers. In addition, because of the shear volume and size of the component, you may have little choice but to house the specific components in multiple containers. Although the number of containers is correct and the demand patterns are linear enough to be on kanban, other kanban container options may be more user friendly for a nonflexible work cell concerned about setup time. This is covered in more detail in the following chapters.

Flexible Work-Cell Production-Card Calculation

Flexible work cells are able to change the *cell production rate* (output of the cell measured as time per piece) by adding and subtracting operators. This keeps the lead time constant. When determining the number of production cards for a flexible work cell, use the highest ADD for which the cell was designed in the formula. If a lower ADD quantity is used, a stock-out will occur when the ADD exceeds the lower ADD that was used to determine the number of cards. The number of kanban cards needed for production is calculated only once, unless the conditions on which it was based change significantly.

$$\text{Number of production kanban cards } = \frac{(\text{Highest ADD}) \, (\text{LT}) \, (1 + .00 \text{ SS})}{(\text{SCC})}$$

The determining feature of a flexible work cell is that it can add or subtract the number of operators to adjust the cell production rate. It is not complicated by long setup times or by machines having to wait for the operator. The lead time is usually determined by industrial engineering if it is a new cell, or by history if it is an existing cell. If you run other components in the same cell, they must be taken into consideration when determining lead times.

Key Points for Calculating the Number of Production Cards

- Apply safety stock when first initiating kanban. You can gradually reduce it as you gain experience. This experience comes in the form of monitoring stock-outs. If stock-outs do not occur, the amount of safety stock can gradually be lowered until stock-outs begin to appear. What usually occurs with the projected average daily demand is that it contains a portion of forecasted demand. In most cases, forecasts are overstated. The amount of overstatement acts as a degree of safety stock, although the input of safety stock is a separate function.

- Add to the manufacturing lead time any additional lead time elements that are required to meet a specific situation (for example, inspection).
- Use this method for determining the number of production cards only as a best guess estimate. The final determination of the number of production cards rests with the production supervisor.

Internal Move Card Calculation

The following formula will calculate the number of internal move cards. *Round trip conveyance lead time* (R.T.C. LT) is used in the calculation and represents the amount of time it takes one internal move card to make one complete round trip from the point of use to the replenishment work cell and back to the point of use with the authorized replenishment. Safety stock is expressed as a decimal (percentage increase: for example, 1.05 = 5% increase).

$$\text{Number of internal move cards} = \frac{\text{(ADD) (R.T.C. LT) (1 + .00 SS)}}{\text{standard container capacity}}$$

To apply this formula you must complete the following three steps:

1. Obtain the ADD for each component.
2. Determine the round trip conveyance lead time.
3. Apply the kanban card formula to determine the preliminary number of internal move kanban cards.

Step 1. Obtain the ADD for each component. In the following example we use part numbers A, B, and C from the initial work-cell production-card calculation.

Part number	Average daily demand
A	480 pieces
B	360 pieces
C	240 pieces

Step 2. Determine the round trip conveyance lead time by using the formula below. This is the amount of time it takes one internal move card to make one complete round trip from the point of use to the replenishment work cell and back to the point of use.

$$\frac{1 \text{ hour R.T.C. LT}}{8 \text{ hours per day available}} = 0.125 \text{ round trip conveyance lead time}$$

Step 3. Apply the following kanban card formula to determine the preliminary number of internal move cards for each part number. Safety stock is expressed as a decimal; for example, 1.05 (5%).

$$\text{Part A} = \frac{(480 \text{ pcs. ADD}) (0.125 \text{ R.T.C. LT}) (1+.00 \text{ SS})}{20\text{-piece standard container capacity}} = 3 \text{ internal move kanban cards}$$

$$\text{Part B} = \frac{(360 \text{ pcs. ADD}) (0.125 \text{ R.T.C. LT}) (1+.00 \text{ SS})}{15\text{-piece standard container capacity}} = 3 \text{ internal move kanban cards}$$

$$\text{Part C} = \frac{(240 \text{ pcs. ADD}) (0.125 \text{ R.T.C. LT}) (1+.00 \text{ SS})}{10\text{-piece standard container capacity}} = 3 \text{ internal move kanban cards}$$

Key Points for Calculating the Number of Internal Move Cards

- The kanban card formula for calculating the number of internal move cards assumes that the internal move card is immediately removed when the container starts to be used and begins its conveyance for replenishment. If the consuming department is on a conveyance schedule (that is, accumulates the internal move cards) and then performs the R.T.C. LT (for example, 1 hour wait time = 0.125 day interval), the collection wait time (CWT) for conveyance must be added to the kanban card formula. In the following example, part C is used to show the wait time.

$$\text{Part C} = \frac{(240 \text{ pcs. ADD}) \ (0.125 \text{ R.T.C. LT} + 0.125 \text{ CWT}) \ (1 + .00 \text{ SS})}{10\text{-piece standard container capacity}} = 6 \text{ internal move kanban cards}$$

- Apply safety stock when you first initiate this system and then gradually reduce it to the point where occasional stock-outs begin to appear.
- Recalculate the quantity of cards when there are changes in
  Average daily demand
  Frequency of conveyance
  Round trip conveyance lead time
- Add any additional lead-time elements to the formula that may be required to meet a specific situation.
- Use this method of ascertaining the number of cards as a best-guess estimate to initiate the system. The production supervisor is responsible for determining the number of cards.

Supplier Card Calculation

Use the supplier kanban card to obtain replenishment from the suppliers. Once consumption begins on the container, the supplier card is removed from the container and placed at a pickup point in the using department. These supplier cards are then collected (collection wait time) throughout the facility on a regular schedule. These cards are then given to the supplier who may, for example, make one trip a day to the facility to pick up cards. If the cards are picked up once a day, the round-trip conveyance lead time would then equal 2 days, which also includes the return trip with the replenishment. Safety stock is expressed as a decimal (for example, 1.05 = 5% increase). The formula for calculating the quantity of supplier kanban cards is shown below:

$$\text{Supplier kanban cards} = \frac{(\text{ADD}) \ (\text{CWT} + \text{R.T.C. LT}) \ (1 + .00 \text{ SS})}{\text{standard container capacity}}$$

Table 2-7. Average Daily Demand for Part Number "D"

Components	ADD	Quantity of part "D" per part	Part "D" ADD
A	480	1 per	480
B	360	1 per	360
C	240	1 per	+240
			1,080 ADD

There are two steps in applying this formula. In the following example we will use part number D, which is a die-cast part that goes into part numbers A, B, and C at a quantity of one per part:

Step 1. Determine the average daily demand for part number D (see Table 2-7).

Step 2. Apply the following particulars to the supplier kanban card formula to determine the number of supplier kanban cards you will need for Part D. In this example you would need 81 supplier kanban cards.

1,080 pieces	=	Average daily demand
1 day	=	Collection wait time: Supplier cards are picked up throughout the shop on a schedule. In this example, it is once a day.
2 days	=	Round-trip conveyance lead time: Supplier makes one trip per day to pick up and deliver.
1.00	=	0% safety stock
40 pieces	=	Standard container capacity

$$\text{Part D} = \frac{(1{,}080 \text{ pcs. ADD}) (1 \text{ day CWT} + 2 \text{ day R.T.C. LT}) (1 + .00 \text{ SS})}{40\text{-piece standard container capacity}} = 81 \text{ supplier kanban cards}$$

Key Points for Calculating the Number of Supplier Kanban Cards

- The supplier kanban card formula above does not cover supplier manufacturing lead time. The supplier in this case maintains a ready supply. If the supplier does not maintain a ready supply or cannot react immediately, his or her lead time for manufacturing, packaging, and so on, must be added to the supplier card kanban formula. In the following example we use 1 day supplier lead time.

$$\text{Part D} = \frac{\overset{\text{1 day}\quad\text{2 day}\quad\;\;\text{1 day}}{(1,080 \text{ pcs. ADD}) (\text{CWT} + \text{R.T.C. LT} + \text{supplier LT}) (1 + .00 \text{ SS})}}{40\text{-piece standard container capacity}} = 108 \text{ supplier kanban cards}$$

- Add to the formula any other elements if they are required by the specific environment. These include

    Receive time (if lengthy)

    Inspection time

    Internal conveyance (if lengthy)

- Apply safety stock when first initiating kanban. You can gradually reduce it as you gain experience. Like calculating the number of production cards, this experience comes in the form of monitoring stock-outs. If stock-outs do not occur, you can gradually lower the amount of safety stock until stock-outs begin to appear. What usually occurs with the projected average daily demand is that it contains a portion of forecasted demand. In most cases, forecasts are over-stated. The amount of overstatement acts as a degree of safety stock, although the input of safety stock is a separate function.

Flexible work-cell staffing formula. Flexible work cells are designed to add or subtract operators when the average daily demand is projected to shift (see Figure 2-7).

As shown in the following formula, to calculate the number of oper-ators you multiply ADD times *labor content per unit* and divide it by the *operator effective time per day*. The labor content per unit encompasses setup time, processing labor time, and move time. The operator effective time per day is the amount of time the operator is producing product. To determine this, take the total time the operator is on-site (typically $8\frac{1}{2}$

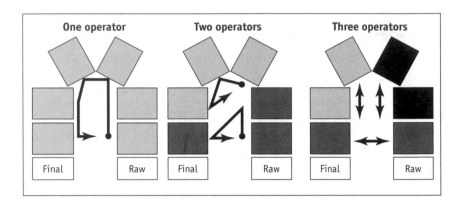

Figure 2-7. Flexible Work Cell Staffing

hours) and subtract lunch, breaks, and other activities such as autonomous maintenance and/or clean up.

$$\text{Number of operators} = \frac{\text{(ADD) (labor content per unit)}}{\text{operator effective time per day}}$$

In the following example, if you project the ADD to be 1,380 pieces
per day, with a labor content per unit of 1 minute, you would require 3
operators. The cell production rate with 3 operators equates to 20 seconds per piece (60 seconds/3 operators) as long as there is no machine
wait time. This means that 1 piece will be completed every 20 seconds.

$$\frac{\text{(1,380 pieces ADD) (1 minute labor content per unit)}}{\text{460 minutes operator effective time per day}} = 3 \text{ operators}$$

If in this example the ADD drops to 920 pieces per day, two operators are required. The cell production rate with 2 workers equates to 30
seconds per piece (60 seconds/2 operators) as long as there is no machine
wait time. This means that one piece is completed every 30 seconds.

$$\frac{\text{(920 pieces ADD) (1 minute labor content per unit)}}{\text{460 minutes operator effective time per day}} = 2 \text{ operators}$$

Once you have calculated the number of production kanban cards, it
will remain constant unless the premise upon which it was calculated

changes significantly. If this occurs, recalculate and adjust the number of production cards accordingly by using the initial production card calculation. What changes from planning period to planning period for flexible work cells is the number of operators, which can be determined with the above formula.

In Chapter 3 we discuss the principles behind the automated kanban system. By combining existing MRPII and manual kanban, you can eliminate most of their non-value-added activities. Card calculations, flexible work cell staffing, and other operations are performed automatically with an automated kanban system, thus giving you the additional benefit of reacting quickly to shifts in customer demand.

3

automated kanban—the automated flow technology

The automated kanban system described in this book is referred to as Automated Flow Technology™ (AFT). (Though AFT is a customized approach to automated kanban, these two terms are used interchangeably throughout the text.) AFT encompasses manufacturing, purchasing, and the supplier base and is a computerized system that interfaces and integrates with the existing MRPII system. It further integrates manual kanban, bar codes, and a simplified version of EDI. By automating and integrating these elements, a company creates an extremely powerful pull system that is highly responsive to customer demand. AFT significantly reduces overall manufacturing cost and enhances customer response time because the non-value-added activities associated with its perpetuation and execution are eliminated or streamlined.

The following chapters give an overview of AFT and explain how it integrates with MRPII, manual kanban, bar codes, and a simplified version of EDI. They also provide readers with the guidelines necessary to develop and write their own AFT program, a program that will interface with most MRPII mainframe or server-based systems.

AUTOMATED FLOW TECHNOLOGY

The AFT system eliminates the non-value-added activities of the manual kanban system by automatically

- Calculating kanban lot sizes
- Creating purchase orders and performing download upon consumption
- Creating and displaying triggered manufacturing orders upon consumption
- Performing receipts
- Calculating flexible work cell staffing

Calculating Kanban Lot Sizes

AFT automatically calculates kanban lot sizes by utilizing *MRP gross requirements* in conjunction with the kanban formula. The automated kanban formula has two additional steps over that of manual kanban:

1. It searches for nonlinear demands and automatically adjusts the kanban lot size accordingly. This is essential, because a nonlinear demand in either a manual or automated kanban system can create a stock-out.
2. Once the new kanban lot size is calculated, AFT will test it by simulating what should actually occur on the shop floor for most of the kanban container options.

AFT performs the simulation using the following elements:

- MRP gross requirements
- On-hand quantities
- Current triggered on-order quantities
- Replenishment lead time

If the kanban lot size fails this simulation test (usually as a result of several medium-sized hits in a row), the AFT program automatically increases the newly calculated kanban lot size and reruns the simulation. These calculation features will help you avert possible stock-outs resulting from projected uneven demand patterns—a situation that can easily occur with manual kanban. A shortcoming of manual kanban is that it operates on the premise of linear usage even though projected demand in most manufacturing environments is not always perfectly linear. By automatically calculating kanban lot sizes and providing simulation capability for most container options, AFT offers some degree of protection beyond manually calculating kanban.

Creating Purchase Orders and Performing Download Upon Consumption

In the kanban system, consumption triggers replenishment via internal move cards, production cards, and supplier cards. One way a company can significantly eliminate non-value-added activities is by automatically creating and downloading purchase orders to suppliers on contracted purchase items. How you create the order is dependent upon the type of container option you employ. An AFT system has four container options:

1. Single-container purchasing
2. Dual-container purchasing
3. Triple-container purchasing
4. Multiple-container purchasing

Single-container purchasing. When the combined total of on-hand plus on-order falls below the kanban lot size, AFT automatically creates and places a purchase order into a hold file pending the supplier download (see Figure 3-1). All the data required to create the purchase order is already stored in MRPII's database. This includes the agreed upon contract price and supplier lead time. When the supplier performs the download at the prescribed time, the AFT system automatically assigns a purchase order number and determines the due date based on the agreed

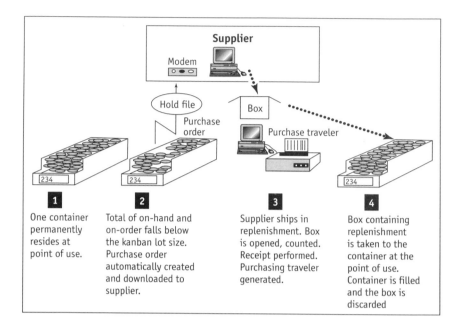

Figure 3-1. Single Container, Purchasing Kanban Replenishment Cycle

upon supplier lead time. In addition to downloading the kanban purchase orders to the suppliers, the MRPII system also provides a one-line-
per-item MRP that is also downloaded for resource planning. The
supplier performs his or her download on a simplified version of electronic data interchange.

Dual-container purchasing. A bar-coded label is permanently affixed
to dual containers. When these containers are empty, the bar code is
scanned by a bar-scanning device located in the shipping department.
This automatically triggers and creates a purchase order by the AFT system, which places it in a hold file pending the supplier download (see
Figure 3-2). Like the single-container option, when the supplier performs
the download at the prescribed time, the AFT system automatically
assigns a purchase order number and determines the due date based on

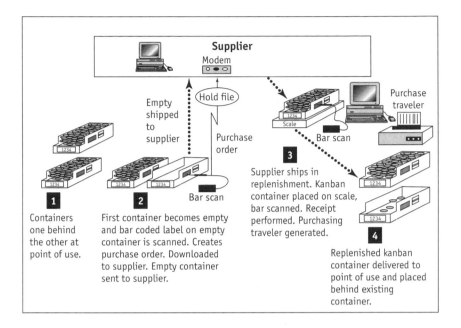

Figure 3-2. Dual Container, Purchasing Kanban Replenishment Cycle

the agreed upon supplier lead time. In addition to downloading the kanban purchase orders to the suppliers, the MRPII system provides a one-line-per-item MRP that is also downloaded for resource planning. The supplier performs the download on a simplified version of electronic data interchange.

Triple-container purchasing. There is also a bar-coded label permanently affixed to the triple container. The method for triggering and creating a purchase order is identical to that for the dual container. With this option, a third empty container resides with the supplier (see Figure 3-3). A company would use this option to minimize the response time for long-distance suppliers. The third container permits the supplier to fill the company's downloaded requirement immediately while the original equipment manufacturer (OEM) is simultaneously shipping an empty

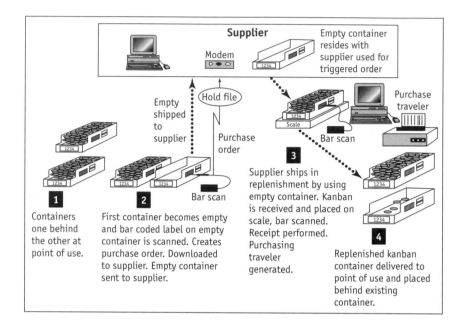

Figure 3-3. Triple Container, Purchasing Kanban Replenishment Cycle

container to the supplier. The supplier performs the download on a simplified version of electronic data interchange. In addition to downloading the kanban purchase orders to the suppliers, the MRPII system also provides a one-line-per-item MRP that is also downloaded for resource planning.

Multiple-container purchasing. The multiple-container option has a plastic packet attached to each container that houses a bar-coded purchasing traveler. When consumption begins on the container, the bar-coded purchase traveler is removed and bar scanned. This automatically creates a purchase order that is placed in a hold file pending the supplier download. Like the single, dual, and triple-container options, when the supplier performs the download at the prescribed time, the AFT system automatically assigns a purchase order number and determines the due

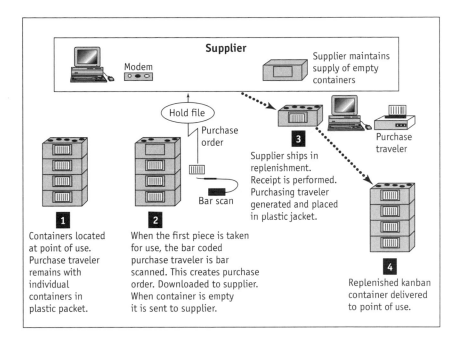

Supplier

Modem

Supplier maintains supply of empty containers

Hold file

Purchase order

Bar scan

3

Supplier ships in replenishment. Receipt is performed. Purchasing traveler generated and placed in plastic jacket.

Purchase traveler

1
Containers located at point of use. Purchase traveler remains with individual containers in plastic packet.

2
When the first piece is taken for use, the bar coded purchase traveler is bar scanned. This creates purchase order. Downloaded to supplier. When container is empty it is sent to supplier.

4
Replenished kanban container delivered to point of use.

Figure 3-4. Multiple Container, Purchasing Kanban Replenishment Cycle

date based on the agreed upon supplier lead time (see Figure 3-4). The supplier performs the download on a simplified version of electronic data interchange. In addition to downloading the kanban purchase orders to the suppliers, the MRPII system provides a one-line-per-item MRP that is also downloaded for resource planning.

Creating and Displaying Triggered Manufacturing Orders Upon Consumption

There are three manufacturing kanban container options: single, dual, and multiple. These are triggered in the same manner as purchasing kanbans (see Figures 3-5, 3-6, and 3-7). However, when a kanban is triggered, the AFT system automatically places it in a *queue file* that is displayed on a computer terminal located at the cell responsible for

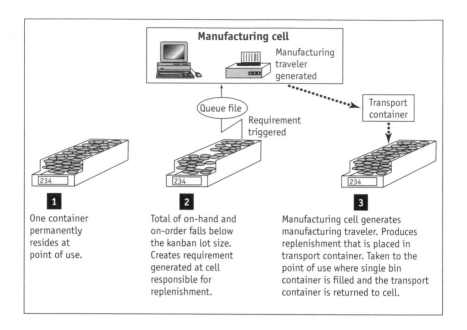

Figure 3-5. Single Container, Manufacturing Kanban Replenishment Cycle

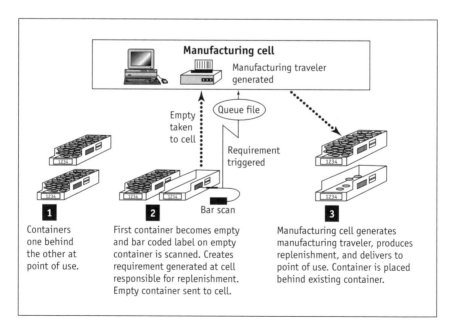

Figure 3-6. Dual Container, Manufacturing Kanban Replenishment Cycle

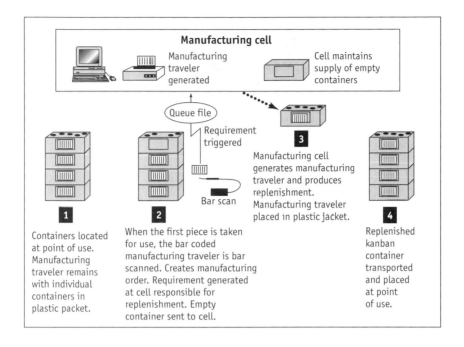

Figure 3-7. Multiple Container, Manufacturing Kanban Replenishment Cycle

replenishment. Before the item is released to be manufactured, AFT automatically runs a *part simulation* to advise the work cell on the availability of supporting components.

When the operator is ready to run the specific item, the AFT system prints a bar-coded manufacturing traveler (see Photo 3-1 and Figure 3-8). This bar-coded traveler is used to initiate (1) deduct points, (2) backflushing, and (3) machine operation. It also provides quality messages and current revision letters. In addition, the bar-coded manufacturing traveler informs the work cell responsible for replenishment where to deliver the completed items. Based upon the ratio of availability of the specific item, you can also apply optional prioritization logic to the triggered kanbans that are in the queue. For example, if the kanban lot size of an item is 100 pieces and there are 30 pieces available, the system will determine that there is a 30% availability. If another part that is pro-

Photo 3-1. Manufacturing Traveler Being Generated at Computer Terminal

Manufacturing Traveler

Part number	10560DEB	Container option	Multiple 6/4
Description	Drive pin assembly	Container size	4S
Quantity	25	Delivery location	Dept. 7/Q9
Due	11/9 08:30 a.m.	Triggered	11/7 08:30 a.m.
Revision	C		

Quality notes: Work station 5—100% inspect radius
                          Work station 6—Check for burr

Note: The system is aware of the number of containers for a given part number (i.e., 6) and how many are currently triggered (i.e., 4).

Figure 3-8. Manufacturing Traveler

duced in the same cell has a 50% availability, AFT places the item with the lowest availability (30%) at the top of the sequential list of how the build should take place. Finally, the current load in hours is visible at all times at the computer terminal located in each work cell.

Performing Receipts

The traditional purchasing receipt process of unpacking and counting the items is time consuming. In addition, non-reusable packaging is expensive. You can eliminate some of this waste by utilizing a reusable egg crate when transporting containers to and from the supplier (see Photo 3-2). In the AFT system, these containers are removed from their egg crates when they arrive at the receiving door and are placed on a modified electronic scale that interfaces with MRPII (see Photo 3-3).

When the containers are bar scanned, the AFT system automatically brings up the purchase order on the screen, determines the number of pieces in the container, compares the part count to the purchase order, transacts the receipt if it is in compliance, and prints a bar-coded *purchase receipt traveler* that indicates where you need to deliver the components (see Figure 3-9). MRPII's database houses information such as the weight of the container, weight of the part, and delivery destination. In some applications, an enlarged picture of the component is on the container, which allows the production floor to perform a visual inspection before putting the material away at the point of use (see Photo 3-4). With the AFT system, items that require inspection are so noted in the routing instruction on the purchase receipt traveler.

Calculating Flexible Work-Cell Staffing

In a pull system, the number of kanban containers remains constant in a flexible work cell while the number of operators are adjusted up or down to compensate for a fluctuation in the average daily demand. AFT handles this by automatically calculating the required number of operators

Photo 3-2. Reuseable Egg Crate

Photo 3-3. Modified Electronic Scale

Purchase Receipt Traveler

Part number _____

Description _____

Quantity
received _____

Date/Time
received _____

Revision _____

Supplier _____

PO
number _____

Quantity
ordered _____

Due date _____

Routing

Inspection—floor location G9

Note: Inspection notes printed (i.e., what to watch for).

Figure 3-9. Purchase Receipt Traveler

Photo 3-4. Photograph of a Component (Enlarged) on the Side of Its Container

each time MRP is exploded. The AFT system does this by first calculating the projected average daily demand using MRP's gross requirements. It then determines staffing levels by using the average daily demand in conjunction with labor content per unit and the operator effective time per day—information that is housed in MRPII.

AUTOMATED FLOW TECHNOLOGY PROGRAMMING

To interface effectively with the current MRPII system, the AFT computerized system requires that you program in-house two separate calculation programs (see Figure 3-10). The first program is the *kanban calculation/simulation program,* and it determines kanban lot sizes. The second program is the *cell staffing calculation program,* and it determines staffing requirements for flexible work cells. An overview of these two computer programs and the required MRPII enhancements are covered in the following sections.

Kanban Calculation/Simulation Program (KCSP)

KCSP is a separate module that you design and program in-house. Its purpose is to calculate kanban lot sizes automatically by accessing MRPII's

- Gross requirements
- Replenishment lead time
- Safety stock setting

KCSP is designed so that once it calculates the kanban lot size for a particular part number, it performs a simulation to determine whether there is a stock-out caused by *spike demands*, *front loads*, or erratic demand patterns. Spike demands are large-quantity requirements that are due beyond replenishment lead time. Front loads are large-quantity requirements that are due within replenishment lead time. Erratic demand patterns lack consistency of requirements from time period to

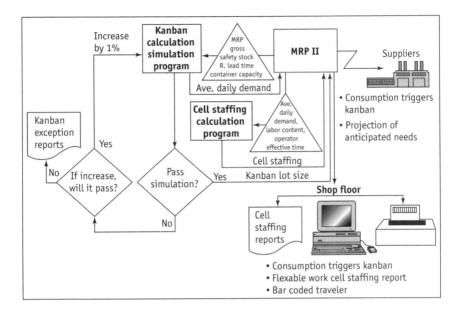

Figure 3-10. Automated Flow Technology System Overview

time period. If the simulation shows that a specific kanban lot size is projected to stock-out because of a spike demand or erratic demand pattern, it automatically increases the kanban lot size by 1% and reruns the simulation. It will continue to run the simulation on these part numbers until it passes—that is, to the point that there is no projected stock-out. If the projected stock-out results from a front load, it will appear on an exception report for further action. Once the particular part number passes the simulation, the kanban lot size is automatically placed in the *item master file* in MRPII. The KCSP performs the simulation program for all container options except for the multiple-container and kanban items that have replenishment lead times of less than a day. This is covered in Chapter 6.

KCSP Programming

You need to program the KCSP module to perform the following five steps:

Step 1. KCSP temporarily halts MRP's gross-to-net explosion calculation when it reaches the *low-level code* (which occurs after all the gross requirements for a specific item have been gathered).

Step 2. KCSP then extracts the gross requirements, replenishment lead times, and safety stock settings from MRPII. KCSP then applies the kanban formula to the gross requirements to calculate the kanban lot size.

Step 3. KCSP runs the kanban lot size through a simulation to determine whether a stock-out occurs. If the kanban lot size passes the simulation, KCSP transfers it to the MRPII item master file. If there is a projected stock-out, the simulation will determine whether an increase in the kanban lot size quantity averts a stock-out. If the answer is "yes," KCSP will increase the kanban lot size by 1% and rerun the simulation. When the kanban lot size finally passes the simulation, it is then transferred to MRPII. If the answer is "no," the projected stock-out is printed out on an exception report for user intervention. Primarily because of timing, adjusting the kanban lot size will not avert a stock-out.

Step 4. After KCSP has determined the kanban lot size, it refers to the *kanban order policy code* to determine how to lot-size the specific part numbers' netted demand. It will then release MRP to complete the gross-to-net explosion calculation it had stopped in step 1. The net requirements will then be offset and lot-sized. KCSP will then release MRP to explode out the next level. This process continues level by level until all components have been addressed.

Step 5. KCSP ascertains the average daily demand for flexible work cells. (This is step 1 of the kanban calculation process. For flexible work cells the KCSP involvement ends here.) The calculated ADD is passed to MRPII's item master file. The cell-staffing program (discussed below) then extracts the ADD for each flexible work cell, kanban part number, labor content per unit, and operator effective time per day to determine the staffing requirements for the flexible work cells after MRP and KCSP are run. The flexible work-cell staffing requirements are then passed to MRPII, which in turn generates a *flexible work-cell staffing report.*

A number of MRP software packages already have the capability to automatically freeze MRP after it has captured the gross requirements. If a particular package does not have this capability, it can be programmed in most cases without changing the original source code by using the following method.

Let us assume that the current MRP that is in production is called MRP A. The user wishes to keep the same source code.

1. A copy of MRP A is made. Name it MRP B. Modify the program of MRP B.
2. The MRP's main procedure should then be modified to reference MRP B. MRP B will now be in production. The management information system (MIS) department thus retains the ability to refer back to MRP A if the need arises. It is, of course, the responsibility of MIS to determine the most effective means for their particular MRPII package.

Cell-Staffing Calculation Programming (CSCP)

Like the KCSP, the CSCP is a separate module that you design and program in-house to calculate the staffing requirements for flexible work cells. This calculation is predicated on

- Average daily demand
- Labor content per unit
- Operator effective time per day

The CSCP module accesses this data from the existing MRPII database once MRP and KCSP have completed their calculations. The labor content per unit is typically drawn from the *router file.* The operator effective time per day is obtained from the *work center master file.* When the average daily demand is automatically determined, the KCSP places it in MRPII's *item master file.* Once CSCP determines the cell staffing requirements, it is automatically placed in a file created by the MIS department in MRPII. This file will then be used in generating a *flexible work-cell staffing report.*

MRPII Enhancements

For the AFT system to interface with your current MRPII system effectively, you need to expand your MRPII program with the following add-on programs and fields:

- Create the ability to generate kanban exception reports.
- Incorporate nine new fields (often accommodated by unused fields).
- Create the ability to obtain required information for the automatic generation of purchase orders once a kanban is triggered.
- Create a temporary hold file for triggered purchase kanban items waiting for supplier download and the calculation and assignment of due dates once the download occurs.
- Create a queue file for triggered manufacturing kanban items at the work cell responsible for replenishment. This includes the ability to obtain and display the required information automatically for the triggered manufacturing item on a computer terminal at the work cell responsible for replenishment.
- Provide simulation of parts availability for triggered manufacturing kanban items prior to releasing them for build.
- Provide an optional prioritization methodology for manufactured kanban items.
- Create the ability to print bar-coded travelers at the work cell responsible for replenishment.
- Create the ability to print the purchase receipt traveler upon receipt of supplier items.

- Create the ability to adjust the number of containers automatically in the multiple-container application.

We discuss these add-on programs in more detail in the following chapters.

The AFT system gives the user flexibility in selecting what items should be handled by kanban and what items should be handled by MRP. This is an important feature of AFT, because not all part numbers are candidates for kanban. Also, implementing kanban is a gradual process. Once you enhance the MRPII system, it will operate not only as it was initially designed, but will automatically calculate and perpetuate a fully automated kanban system as well. Programming the KCSP and CSCP modules and the MRPII enhancements should take between 20 to 25 person-days.

LEAD-TIME DEFINITIONS FOR THE AFT SYSTEM

The AFT system has four lead-time fields: (1) supplier, (2) purchasing replenishment, (3) manufacturing, and (4) manufacturing replenishment. Each of these lead-time fields has a specific application.

Supplier Lead Time

The supplier lead time is the contractual, agreed upon lead time required for the supplier to deliver the goods to the user's facility once the supplier has received the download from the OEM. The supplier lead time is used to calculate the supplier due date once the download occurs. With the dual-container application, the supplier lead time must take into account the extra transit time for the supplier to receive empty containers. In the single-container application, there are no containers in transit; in the triple-container application, an empty container already resides with the supplier; in the multiple-container application, the supplier has empty unassigned containers.

Purchasing Replenishment Lead Time

The purchasing replenishment lead time is the amount of time accumulated to signal a need for replenishment and to obtain and deliver it to
the point of use (see Figure 3-11). The elements needed for determining
purchasing replenishment lead times include the following:

- *OEM's delay time in generating a triggered kanban signal:*
  Figure 3-11 shows that deduct-points throughout the OEM's
  work cells are placed one hour apart. This impacts a single-
  container option, in which consumption is not registered
  immediately.
- *Longest interval between scheduled downloads:* In the example in Figure 3-11, the supplier agrees to download requirements once a day.
- *Supplier lead time:* Figure 3-11 shows that the supplier
  agrees to deliver replenishment two days after receiving
  download.
- *Maximum receiving, inspection, transport to point of use, and
  put away:* In Figure 3-11, this is seven hours.

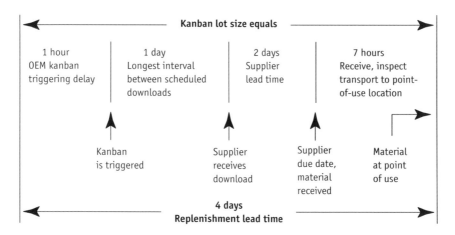

Figure 3-11. Purchasing Replenishment Lead Time Elements

In this example, you would use the total purchasing replenishment lead time of four days to calculate kanban lot sizes and perform simulations on the newly calculated kanban lot sizes.

Manufacturing Lead Time

Manufacturing lead time is the amount of time it takes the work cell to manufacture the component. The due date that is printed on the manufacturing traveler is calculated from the manufacturing lead time. For dual containers, you must transport frequently so as not to lengthen the manufacturing lead time.

Manufacturing Replenishment Lead Time

Manufacturing replenishment lead time is the amount of time accumulated to signal a need for replenishment and to manufacture and deliver it to the point of use (see Figure 3-12). It encompasses the following elements:

- *OEM's delay time in generating a triggered kanban signal:* In the example in Figure 3-12, deduct-points on the work cells are placed one hour apart in a single-container option and do not register consumption immediately. Delay time equals one hour.
- *Longest interval between scheduled downloads to the work cell responsible for replenishment:* This is usually performed immediately.
- *Manufacturing lead time:* In this example, 1.8 days.
- *Transport replenishment to the point of use and put away:* In this example, 0.075 per day.

In this example, you would use the total manufacturing replenishment lead time of two days to calculate kanban lot sizes and perform simulations on the newly calculated kanban lot sizes.

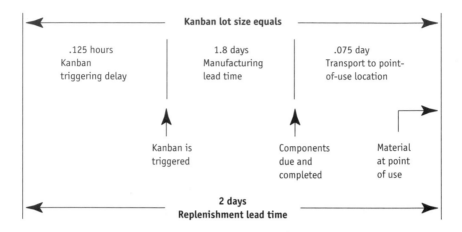

Figure 3-12. Manufacturing Replenishment Lead Time Elements

KANBAN LOT SIZE VERSUS KANBAN ORDER QUANTITY

There is a distinction between the kanban lot size and *kanban order quantity*. The calculated kanban lot size must be of a quantity that supports continued usage until the triggered demand is received, whereas the kanban order quantity can be a fraction of the kanban lot size, as in the case of a multiple-container application, or equal to the full kanban lot size, as in the case of a dual- or triple-container application.

The calculated kanban lot size is never less than the ADD multiplied by the purchasing or manufacturing replenishment lead time. If, for example, the ADD is 200 pieces per day and the purchasing replenishment lead time is five days, the calculated kanban lot size cannot be less than 1,000 pieces. When a kanban is triggered for replenishment, the initial 1,000 pieces on hand permit continued use of the item until the replenishment arrives.

KANBAN ORDER POLICY CODE

After KCSP determines the final kanban lot size, MRPII will refer to the order policy code to determine how to apply the kanban lot size to the net requirements. The following are the four kanban order policy codes.

1. *Single-container discrete policy code:* MRP employs a discrete (one for one) lot sizing for the single-container discrete policy code. Each time the combined total of on-hand plus on-order quantity drops below the kanban lot size, the difference is ordered. For example, if your kanban lot size for a particular part number is 600 and the combined total of on-hand and on-order is 580 pieces, 20 pieces would be ordered.

2. *Single-container full policy code:* MRP employs the full kanban lot size when lot-sizing for the single-container full policy code. When the kanban is triggered, the order quantity will be for the full kanban lot size.

3. *Dual- and triple-container policy code:* MRP employs the full kanban lot size when lot-sizing for the dual- and triple-container policy code. When the order quantity is triggered, it will also be for the full kanban lot size.

4. *Multiple-container policy code:* The lot sizing employed by MRP will be rounded to the number of pieces the standard container is assigned to hold. When the order quantity is triggered, it will also be for the number of pieces that the standard container is assigned to hold.

SUPPLIER DOWNLOAD CAPABILITY

Obtaining downloading capability with your supplier through the electronic data interchange (EDI) may not be the proper approach. The OEM should always query their supplier base before obtaining this capability. They may find that only a few of their suppliers have EDI capability. There is a less expensive, highly effective method of transmitting triggered kanban orders and one-line-per-item MRP projections to your suppliers. All the supplier needs is a personal computer, modem, and off-the-shelf telecommunication software that costs less than $150.00. Many off-the-shelf programs can handle this task. Once the program is in-stalled, the OEM merely has to give the suppliers a password to access the OEM's computer so that the suppliers can download their data. This method is relatively easy to set up and use.

The Automated Flow Technology™ system is designed to eliminate the non-value-added activities inherent in present-day replenishment systems. It is a pull system that is programmed to react swiftly to shifts in demand at minimal cost. Yet replenishment systems are only as effec-tive as the manufacturing processes and suppliers that they serve. Little benefit is achieved by implementing kanban without first implementing the prerequisites of kanban—the subject of the next chapter. Only when all these elements are in place and united with AFT will you create a world class manufacturing environment.

4

kanban prerequisites—WCM techniques

You can implement kanban prior to other world-class manufacturing (WCM) techniques as long as (1) you are prepared to carry large amounts of safety stock to compensate for the inefficiencies of your facility and your suppliers, (2) the cost of the internal and external inefficiencies is not a concern, and (3) response time to customer requirements is not a priority. Kanban can function without improvement to the operation or supplier base, but the time and effort to implement kanban will usually yield little benefit without first putting in place the other WCM techniques. Kanban is but one tool among many WCM techniques—alone it cannot create a world-class manufacturing environment. Although the non-value-added activities from an ineffective replenishment system negatively impact the reaction capability and drive up the cost of the product, they are of secondary concern compared to the benefits that you will derive from implementing the other WCM techniques first. To realize the full potential of kanban, you must implement its prerequisites. In implementing these prerequisites, you need to focus on the following three kanban objectives that clearly demonstrate the interrelationship of kanban to the other WCM techniques:

1. Reducing manufacturing and supplier replenishment lead times
2. Reducing batch sizes

3. Rectifying obstacles that can impede replenishment performance

OBJECTIVE ONE: REDUCE MANUFACTURING AND SUPPLIER REPLENISHMENT LEAD TIMES

When you reduce manufacturing/purchasing replenishment lead times you are reducing inventory, freeing up floor space, and simplifying the perpetuation of the kanban system. Each container option experiences a different impact as a result of long replenishment lead times.

Single-container discrete application. When a part number is placed on a single-container discrete option, the AFT system continuously compares the total of on-hand and on-order quantities to the kanban lot size. When this combined total falls below the kanban lot size, a replenishment order is automatically launched for the difference. The longer the manufacturing/supplier replenishment lead time, the greater the number of orders at any one point in time (see Figure 4-1). Dealing with a significant number of orders becomes cumbersome. The ultimate goal is to reduce the manufacturing/supplier replenishment lead time to the point that you can employ a broadcast methodology.

Single-container, full kanban lot size/dual- and triple-container application. The greater the replenishment lead time, the higher the inventory levels. In these kanban container/order applications, the average inventory carried is one-half the order quantity (see Figure 4-2).

Multiple-container application. The longer the replenishment lead time, the greater the number of containers required in the replenishment loop (see Figure 4-3). From the standpoint of space, perpetuation, maintenance, and prioritizing, dealing with many containers becomes cumbersome. The shorter the replenishment lead time, the fewer containers in the loop and the better the visibility.

Single Container—Discrete Application

Part number 1253
5 day manufacturing replenishment lead time = 45 open orders end of day five

Time of day	Consumption occurred					Triggered order due				
	Day 1	Day 2	Day 3	Day 4	Day 5	Day 6	Day 7	Day 8	Day 9	Day 10
07:00 a.m.	5	5	5	5	5	5	5	5	5	5
08:00 a.m.	5	5	5	5	5	5	5	5	5	5
09:00 a.m.	5	5	5	5	5	5	5	5	5	5
10:00 a.m.	5	5	5	5	5	5	5	5	5	5
11:00 a.m.	5	5	5	5	5	5	5	5	5	5
12:00 p.m.	5	5	5	5	5	5	5	5	5	5
01:00 p.m.	5	5	5	5	5	5	5	5	5	5
02:00 p.m.	5	5	5	5	5	5	5	5	5	5
03:00 p.m.	5	5	5	5	5	5	5	5	5	5

45 piece average daily demand—Kanban lot size = 225

Part number 1253
2 day manufacturing replenishment lead time = 18 open orders end of day two

Time of day	Consumption occurred		Triggered order due	
	Day 1	Day 2	Day 3	Day 4
07:00 a.m.	5	5	5	5
08:00 a.m.	5	5	5	5
09:00 a.m.	5	5	5	5
10:00 a.m.	5	5	5	5
11:00 a.m.	5	5	5	5
12:00 p.m.	5	5	5	5
01:00 p.m.	5	5	5	5
02:00 p.m.	5	5	5	5
03:00 p.m.	5	5	5	5

45 piece average daily demand—Kanban lot size = 90

Figure 4-1. Manufacturing/Supplier Replenishment Lead Time Influences the Number of Open Orders

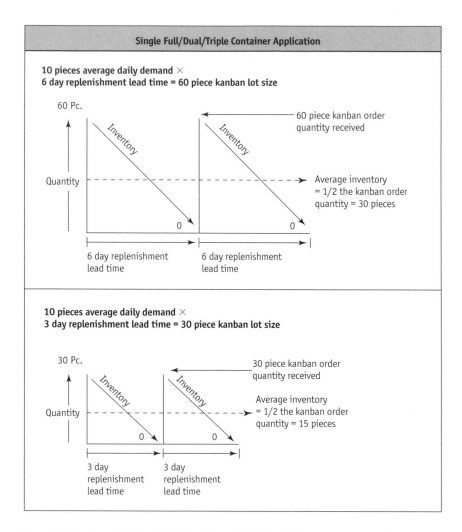

Figure 4-2. Manufacturing/Supplier Replenishment Lead Time Influences Inventory Levels

Multiple Container Application
100 pieces average daily demand $\times$ 6 day replenishment lead time = 600 piece kanban lot size
Production cards $= \dfrac{(100 \text{ pcs. ave. daily}) \textbf{(6 day replenishment lead time)} (1 + \text{safety stock})}{50 \text{ piece container}} = \textbf{12 cards}$
100 pieces average daily demand $\times$ 3 day replenishment lead time = 300 piece kanban lot size
Production cards $= \dfrac{(100 \text{ pcs. ave. daily}) (3 \text{ day replenishment lead time}) (1+ \text{safety stock})}{50 \text{ piece container}} = \textbf{6 cards}$

Figure 4-3. Replenishment Lead Time Influences the Number of Containers

OBJECTIVE TWO: REDUCE BATCH SIZES

Long setup times force deviation from the intended methodology of properly sequencing triggered kanban and inflate the calculated kanban with minimum run quantities. In other words, long setup times force deviation of making what is needed, when needed, in the quantity needed. For example, when a multiple container is triggered, it should not be forced to be batched or sequenced with similar families of parts to save on setup time. Long setup times force the use of minimum run quantities that override the much smaller kanban lot size calculation. The overall impact is inflated inventory, problems with prioritizing, increased lead times, and lack of flexibility.

OBJECTIVE THREE: RECTIFY POTENTIAL OBSTACLES THAT CAN IMPEDE REPLENISHMENT PERFORMANCE

The kanban formula uses replenishment lead time in its calculation to ascertain the kanban lot sizes. This allows enough inventory to be on-hand until replenishment arrives. If replenishment does not arrive within the manufacturing/purchasing replenishment lead time, a stock-out is likely to occur. The following factors can prevent attainment of replenishment within lead time:

- Long setup times
- Weak supplier base
- Lack of training
- Machine breakdowns
- Quality issues
- Disorganized workplace
- Data integrity issues

In the remainder of this chapter and in Chapter 5, we discuss the many programs, techniques, and tools that make up the kanban prerequisites to realize the three kanban objectives.

KANBAN PREREQUISITES

Kanban prerequisites significantly reduce the supplier/manufacturing replenishment lead time, reduce batch sizes, and rectify potential obstacles that can impede timely delivery. Proper application of these prerequisites combined with the AFT system can significantly enhance customer response time, lower inventories, and substantially reduce costs. These prerequisites include the following:

- World class manufacturing conversion plan
- Just-in-time education
- Total productive maintenance program
- Quick changeover program
- Zero quality control
- Visual workplace (5S)
- Focused factory/work cells
- Backflushing/deduct-point capability
- Stockroom elimination
- Performance measurements
- Container selection
- Supplier performance rating and contracts
- Data integrity

World Class Manufacturing Conversion Plan

Implementing world class manufacturing (or lean production) must be guided by strategic objectives that clearly define

1. What must be accomplished
2. When it must be accomplished
3. Why it must be accomplished (to be explained to the people)

This process includes

- Analyzing external and internal factors
- Identifying specifically what must be accomplished and by when
- Identifying the specific techniques that need to be applied
- Establishing baseline measurements
- Providing education
- Constructing a detailed implementation milestone chart
- Developing and implementing on-going measurements

It takes a number of years to implement WCM techniques fully, and you must apply them first to those areas that can best aid the company to be competitive. The following steps are a guideline to developing a WCM conversion plan:

1. Benchmark company performance levels against competitors.
2. Understand the strengths and weaknesses of the competition.
3. Define strategic objectives to be achieved. They should be few, clearly stated, and measurable. Examples include reducing the lead time of product to customer from two weeks to three days by March 1999; reducing the cost of goods sold from $5,200 per unit to $3,500 by January of 2000.
4. Explain to the entire work force what goals the company needs to accomplish and why.
5. Train all employees on JIT and other process-improvement

techniques. This minimizes the resistance to change and enables them to accomplish the strategic objectives.

6. Take managers, team leaders, operators, and other personnel on plant tours of world class manufacturing sites. Good will, ideas, and inspiration will be gained.

7. Assess your operation including the supplier base to determine specifically what must be changed to accomplish the strategic objectives. Examples include eliminating the non-value-added steps in the manufacturing process and reducing machine down time.

8. Determine the specific world class manufacturing techniques that should be implemented to accomplish your strategic objectives. For example, you might need to implement a focus factory encompassing work cells and total productive maintenance.

9. Assess the organization chart. Usually business units are created by product line encompassing the required positions to run the area as a self-contained unit.

10. Assess the required skill levels of each position in the business unit that are necessary to perpetuate the business unit on a daily basis and to implement and perpetuate the world class manufacturing techniques. These required skills are then compared to your present personnel. Train personnel in those skills that are missing and/or hire new personnel.

11. Develop a detailed implementation milestone chart reflecting each step required to implement the specific improvement in the process. This should specify the activities that are to be performed, where, by whom, and when.

12. Set progressive numeric goals. Put on-going measurements in place.

13. Train the team leaders how to perform cost-benefit analysis.

Implementation that does not yield a satisfactory pay-back should be questioned.

14. Track and discuss the progress of the implementation milestone chart at least weekly in team meetings.

15. Standardize the methodologies as each area implements the required changes. Train the people accordingly.

16. Follow up to ensure that the process-changes and new methodologies that you have implemented are being used and perpetuated as designed. Monitor actual performance levels to the progressive goals that were set. Adjust processes and methodologies where required.

Implementing kanban has its place in the WCM implementation milestone chart, and, in fact, is the tool designed for managing and ensuring just-in-time production. However, since kanban's effectiveness depends on the strength of the organization and supplier base, it is not usually one of the first items put into place. You need to address many issues before you can create an environment in which kanban operates effectively. The following educational programs, WCM techniques, and good business practices are used to create this environment.

Just-in-Time Education

Just-in-time production is one of the two cornerstones of the Toyota production system. When applied to a single industrial process, the JIT concept means making items when they are required and in the quantities required, all as inexpensively as possible. This is done by minimizing inventory, synchronizing production processes, and producing in a continuous stream with a minimum of work in process. To deal with high-diversity, low-volume reduction through the JIT approach, a company must abandon large lots in favor of smaller lots and level production.[1]

JIT is much more than an inventory reduction system. It encompasses much more than reducing changeover, using kanban, or modernizing the factory. As Mr. Ohno, the father of the Toyota production system says, it is "making a factory operate for the company just like the human body operates for an individual." In a flow process operating under the JIT approach, the right parts needed in assembly reach the assembly line at the time they are needed and only in the amount needed. A company establishing this flow throughout can approach zero inventory.[2]

To be successful in a WCM environment, everyone within a facility needs to participate in the implementation and perpetuation of JIT. To accomplish this, everyone in the company should be trained in JIT. Training is the key that breaks down resistance—people will naturally resist what they do not understand. Each employee should also understand how all the techniques integrate and complement each other.

For example, a well-constructed work cell can be ineffective if the machines continuously break down, defective parts are being produced, or the work cell is disorganized and cluttered. Many techniques come together to make the work cell effective; therefore, employees must fully understand all the techniques and tools needed to convert to a WCM environment. From an overall perspective, employees should understand why it is important to

1. Produce to customer demand versus producing to forecast
2. Eliminate waste
3. Pull rather than push
4. Have the machines be highly effective
5. Produce quality product each and every time
6. Produce with a lot size of one
7. Continuously improve
8. Have measurements
9. Have a close working relationship with the supplier base

The technical training should include the following tools and processes:

- Total productive maintenance
- Quick changeover
- Focused factory/work cells
- Zero defects
- Visual workplace
- Kanban

Many companies adopt a formal training program that gives each employee a prescribed number of training hours to acquire and maintain skill levels. The higher the skill level of each employee, the greater the competitive advantage of the company.

Total Productive Maintenance (TPM) Program

TPM is an innovative approach to maintenance that optimizes equipment effectiveness, eliminates breakdowns, and promotes autonomous operator maintenance through day-to-day activities involving the total work force. TPM promotes group activities throughout the organization for greater equipment effectiveness and trains operators to share responsibility with maintenance personnel for routine inspection, cleaning, maintenance, and minor repairs. Over time, this cooperative effort dramatically increases productivity and quality, optimizes equipment life cycle cost, and broadens the base of every employee's knowledge and skills. To be effective, TPM must be implemented on a companywide basis.[3] TPM embodies the following integrated strategies to elevate the performance of the machines:

Preventive maintenance. Maintenance is performed predicated upon mean time between failures (MTBF). On this level, the machines are maintained to perform at traditional levels. Under preventive maintenance, machine breakdowns still occur and unnecessary repairs are performed. Preventive maintenance, however, is more effective than breakdown maintenance. It is estimated that machines that unexpectedly break down cost three times more to repair than a scheduled repair.

Autonomous maintenance. The performance of the machines is elevated by involving the operators to perform daily checks, cleaning, and lubrication of the machines. Equipment operators also eliminate the source of contamination, implement visual controls, and participate in analyzing and rectifying the six big losses of machine ineffectiveness:

1. Breakdowns
2. Setup and adjustment loss
3. Idling and minor stoppages
4. Reduced speed
5. Defects and rework
6. Startup and yield loss

If a company is already practicing preventive maintenance, TPM can be adopted easily by adding autonomous maintenance by operators to the existing system. If a company has not yet implemented preventive or productive maintenance, a sudden shift from breakdown maintenance to TPM is extremely difficult.[4]

Predictive maintenance. Predictive maintenance can be expensive and is used only on critical machines. This method relies on assessing the actual condition of the machine as opposed to MTBF. Monitoring techniques to diagnose the actual condition of the machine and to identify signs of deterioration or imminent failure include the following:

1. *Vibration analysis* uses nonintrusive sensing devices to measure the vibration of the machine, as there is a correlation between the machine's vibration and its current condition. This information is monitored for trends via a computer to ascertain the current and projected (trending) condition of the machine and to determine when repairs need to be performed.
2. *Thermography* measures heat emissions and looks for abnormalities in electrical equipment.

3. *Tribology* ascertains wear patterns by analyzing the oil of the machine.

Overall equipment effectiveness (OEE) measurement. TPM uses an index called OEE to measure and gauge the effectiveness of the machine. The formula for determining the OEE is

$$OEE = availability \times performance \times quality$$

The OEE measurement will provide you with the following information:

- It reflects where the machine stands in relationship to a world-class performance benchmark of 85%.
- It guides the user to the specific areas that require improvement, as it provides the individual measurement of down time, speed losses, and defects, as well as an overall measurement.
- It lends itself to goal-setting comparison to actual performance to determine whether progress is being made.

TPM's goal is zero failures and zero defects. By ensuring the efficiency, accuracy, ease of operation and maintenance, and availability of equipment and systems, TPM improves the uptime and performance of the machines, and in turn significantly improves obtaining replenishment within lead time.

Quick Changeover Program

To achieve just-in-time effectively, it is necessary to have quick changeover. Quick changeover comes from SMED, the acronym for Single-Minute Exchange of Die (or single-minute setup), developed by Shigeo Shingo. It is a simple and universal approach that works in companies all over the world. The basic principles of quick changeover can be used to reduce setup and turnaround time in all types of manufacturing, assembly, and even service industries, from process and packaging plants to airlines.[5]

Quick changeover significantly reduces setup times from hours to minutes. The first attempt in its application usually results in a 50% reduction in setup time with little or no expenditures. Quick changeover means thinking about changeover in a new way. Shigeo Shingo, the developer of SMED, learned a great deal by simply observing what people did during changeover and thinking carefully about how the necessary setup work could be done with the shortest possible downtime.[6] Because what you learn on one machine can usually be applied to other machines, quick changeover affords rapid improvement throughout the facility. These are the basic steps:

1. Videotape the entire setup operation.
2. Show the video to the machine operators prior to others viewing and working with the tape. This is not only a courtesy that fosters trust, but it frequently leads to improvement on its own as the operator realizes from the tape where immediate improvements can easily be made.
3. Identify the individual elements of the setup to determine whether they are currently internal or external. This is the most important step in quick changeover. The main reason traditional setup operations take so long is that internal and external aspects of setup are confused. Internal setup consists of those activities that must be performed while the machine is shut down (as, for example, to remove a tool). External setup consists of those activities that can be performed while the machine is running (as in presetting the tools for the next job).
4. Identify those elements that are currently internal that can be moved or converted to external.
5. Eliminate and streamline as many of the remaining internal elements as you can.

6. Eliminate and streamline as many of the external elements as you can.

7. Eliminate adjustments and test runs, which account for a large portion of the setup time.

In some cases you can eliminate the need for the setup altogether through redesigning the component or by dedicating spare equipment. In any case, long setup times can be challenged and reduced, thus permitting the work cell to respond to triggered kanbans without concern for setups or minimum run quantities.

Quick changeovers also make daily production work go smoother because there is less physical strain or risk of injury. Less inventory makes production easier and safer with less clutter in the workplace. Setup tools are standardized and combined, so there are fewer tools to keep track of.[7] The quick changeover technique should be applied both to the OEM's facility and the supplier base.

Zero Quality Control

The dual goals of TPM are zero breakdowns and zero defects. Zero defects means catching and fixing human mistakes and machine errors before they can cause defects. Zero quality control (ZQC) was used by Japanese companies for many years. It was one of the secrets of low-inventory production, since no defects means no need for buffer inventory to replace defective products. ZQC can eliminate wastes related to quality defects—rework, scrap, and equipment downtime—and maintain the company's competitiveness. It also makes production and assembly work easier. One of the great things about ZQC is that it focuses on correcting the conditions for processing, not on blaming people for making mistakes. Shigeo Shingo, the developer of ZQC, recognized that it is human nature to make mistakes or forget things. People should not be punished for mistakes. Punishment only makes people feel bad—it does not eliminate defects.[8] ZQC employs a number of techniques aimed at producing a quality product each and every time:

Standardization. This is a method for stabilizing performance by reducing variability created by people, machines, tools, material, measures, and information. Standards can be written or pictorial and should be made visible to all concerned. Since these standards are based upon scientific methods and technology, you should develop them expressly for those who will use and understand them.

Poka-yoke (or mistake-proofing). This is a method of mistake-proofing at the source by using mechanical means and electrical sensing devices to prevent defects from occurring—before they cause defects. It takes the immediate action of stopping operations when an error is detected, such as by installing an interlocked circuit that automatically shuts down the machine. In poka-yoke, the design of the product and its components are also analyzed and design modifications are made to minimize potential manufacturing errors. In keeping with the spirit of poka-yoke, the design refinement process should incorporate the experiences of the production workers, since they are in the best position to discover design elements that cause difficulty but serve no value-added function.[9]

Many things can go wrong in the complex environment of the workplace; every day there are opportunities to make mistakes that will result in defective products. Defects are wasteful, and if they are not discovered, they disappoint the customer's expectations of quality. Behind poka-yoke is the conviction that it is not acceptable to produce even a small number of defective goods. To become a world class competitor, a company must adopt not only a philosophy but a practice of producing zero defects. Poka-yoke methods are simple concepts for achieving this goal.[10]

Analytical tools. A full armament of tools are employed to analyze defects and to determine and rectify the cause. Examples include check sheets, pareto diagrams, histograms, and cause-and-effect diagrams.

Achieving a high level of quality is paramount in applying a kanban system. The goal of JIT is to eliminate waste, thus reducing cost, customer response time, and inventories.

Visual Workplace

A visual workplace is visually organized, displayed, and controlled. Work standards are apparent to everyone, and abnormalities can be recognized at a glance. The condition of the plant is such that a visitor can walk into any area within the plant and understand everything that is going on within five minutes.

The method of achieving a visual workplace begins with 5S, which stands for

- Sort (organization): Identify what is not required.
- Set in order (orderliness): Determine a place for everything and put everything in its place.
- Shine (cleanliness): Clean and develop methods to keep it clean.
- Standardize: Develop and implement standards throughout the workplace.
- Sustain (self-discipline): Stick to the rules; develop good habits.

These are simple activities that can be difficult to implement. 5S-ing entails far more than simply cleaning up; it must be in place prior to any successful development of JIT or TPM.

The advantages of a visual workplace are as follows:

1. It is highly effective in helping everyone recognize abnormalities.
2. Operators can control their own activities more easily.
3. It helps create higher productivity.
4. It produces fewer defects.
5. It helps workers meet deadlines.
6. The plant sells itself to the customers.

A visual workplace creates an environment conducive to perpetuating an effective kanban system.

Focused Factory/Work Cells

Focused factories are self-contained business units (product family groupings) that are physically organized for an efficient flow of materials. Within each focus factory are a number of individual work cells, each producing components or assemblies that feed into a final assembly process. The objective of the focused factory is to minimize the travel distance between the individual work cells. The objective of the work cell is to place all the machinery and supporting elements required (for example, tooling, required material) in a self-contained area to produce the required item(s). The goal of focused factory/work cells is to minimize waste and gain the capability to produce to a quantity of one. There are basically two types of work cells: the *component work cell* and the *subassembly/assembly work cell*.

Component work cell. The component work cell consists of dissimilar machinery that is tightly fitted and arranged by sequence of operation. The operator is skilled in each of these machines and operates more than one at a time. The cell is flexible in that you can add or subtract personnel as the demand fluctuates (see Figure 2-7 on page 40). The ideal lot size through these cells is a quantity of one. This permits a quick through-put time.

Subassembly/assembly work cell. The subassembly/assembly work cell's flexibility and response time is enhanced significantly through the elimination of kiting (stock room pulls), which is a non-value-added activity. You can accomplish this by moving the item to be assembled to where the parts are located (point of use) within the cell (see Photo 4-1). The material is arranged by sequence of assembly. Products that have large components are handled by use of a gravity conveyor that feeds from behind the work cell. Having high visibility of performance is important for work cell control (see Photo 4-2). Various methods are used

Photo 4-1. Material Located at Point of Use

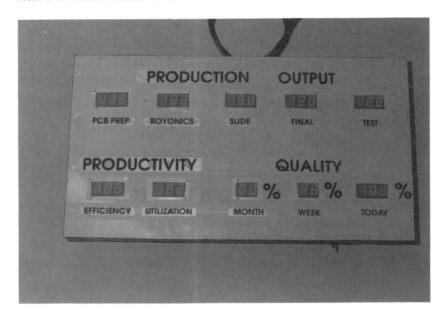

Photo 4-2. Visual Workplace Control Board

This visual workplace electronic board is updated every two minutes. The units being made are bar scanned at each deduct point to update. Also, the test station automatically registers the quality.

depending upon the size and complexity of the work cell. Naturally, the size of the containers kept at the point of use affects the size of the cell.

Using the focused factory concept with work cells significantly reduces waste and lead time. Manufacturing replenishment lead times can often be reduced from weeks to a matter of hours. This favorably impacts kanban by reducing inventory and minimizing the number of triggered orders in the replenishment loop.

Backflushing/Deduct Point Capability

Many OEM's have stockrooms that store components, subassemblies, assemblies, and final product. Under this method, a material planner determines what needs to be built per the MRP and creates and releases a *job packet* to the stockroom. The job packet includes a pick-list for items that need to be pulled from the stockroom and sent to the production floor. Once the pick-list has been pulled, it is entered in the computer. What has been picked is subtracted from the inventory and any shortages are inputted. After everything has been entered in the computer, the kit consisting of what has been taken from the stockroom is then released to the production staging area, where it is kept until all the parts are available or until there is sufficient capacity to start the build. Since this process is time-consuming, the OEM tries to compensate by making the kit sizes large, thus encouraging batch building.

The alternative method as described above is to construct work cells with material located at the point of use. At the beginning of the work cell is a computer terminal and printer. When a kanban is triggered through consumption, a bar-coded traveler is generated at the cell responsible for replenishment—if all the supporting components are simulated to be available. Once the item is made, the bar-coded manufacturing traveler is bar-scanned and the quantity produced is entered into the computer. The system then performs transactions referred to as *backflushing,* which will

- Subtract (decrement) from the on-hand inventory the specific components and quantities that were used in building the parent part number.
- Increase (increment) the parent part number's on-hand balance.
- Subtract (decrement) the running total of what is on-order for the parent part number. The on-order quantity for a specific parent number is automatically increased when a bar-coded traveler is generated and then subtracted upon completion.

You should slightly alter this approach if deduct points are used. *Deduct points* are intermediate points of completion. They are used to subtract the on-hand inventory of components that have been applied to the partially completed parent up to a specific point in the assembly process. You initiate this transaction by bar scanning the bar-coded number and keying in the quantity of assemblies that come across each of the deduct points. This will

- Subtract the on-hand inventory of components that have been applied to the assembly process up to that specific point.
- Increase a *bucketed work-in-process* file of those parts and quantities that have been subtracted from the on-hand inventory.

Upon completion, the backflush takes over and performs four functions:

1. Relieves the bucketed work-in-process file of parts and quantities that have been subtracted from the on-hand inventory.
2. Subtracts from the on-hand inventory any components that were not covered by the deduct points—usually from the last deduct point to the backflush point.
3. Increases the parent part number on-hand balance.

4. Subtracts the running total of what is on-order for the parent part number.

From a kanban perspective, the purpose of the deduct points for when long processes are involved is to allow for quick notification of the use of components to the Automated Flow Technology™ (AFT). This is an early response mechanism in triggering single-container kanbans that also simplifies the cycle-counting process. Figure 4-4 demonstrates the placement of deduct points and backflushing locations in a work cell. The spacing of deduct points in the cell can be manufacturing-time-related (for example, spaced 15 minutes apart) throughout all the cells. Consistency throughout the facility simplifies the process of determining manufacturing replenishment lead time.

Stockroom Elimination

The stockroom is the single largest non-value-added function in the manufacturing process. The expense of operating a stockroom is enormous. You must take into account overhead, personnel, handling equipment, computer input time, and expedite time. What you get in return is extended lead times, forced batch runs due to pick time (the time it takes to pull a kit), double and triple handling of material, increased lead time, and inflexibility. You can eliminate the stockroom as soon as work cells, backflushing, and deduct points are in place. There are six steps involved in eliminating the stockroom:

1. *Change the location of the parts physically and in the computer and place them in the new work cell locations.* These parts should be located at or near the point of use.
2. *Place the parts in containers.* Position these parts in an assembly work cell in front of the assembler for easy access.
3. *Place an overflow rack in each area to accommodate components that do not fit in their assigned containers.* In the initial phase of disbanding the stockroom some of the

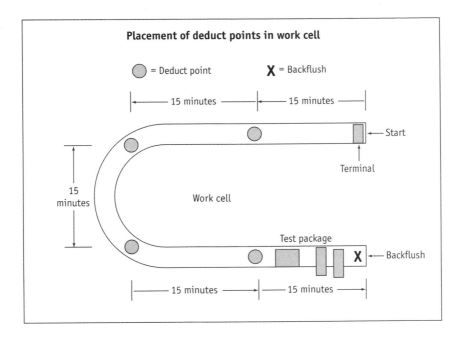

Figure 4-4. Deduct Points Are Evenly Spaced by Time

components will not fit in their assigned containers (in front of the assemblers) because of high inventory levels. When implementing kanban, place a sticker on the kanban container indicating that material is available on the overflow rack. This will prevent a premature triggering of an empty kanban container.

4. *Program the MRPII system to generate a purchasing receipt traveler when performing a traditional purchase receipt.* This will direct the delivery of components to where the components are housed on the manufacturing floor. You will also use this feature when the purchased items are placed on kanban.

5. *Provide computer terminals and printers at each manufacturing cell so that the floor personnel can*

- Determine where to deliver the completed item. This will be the floor location where the material is stored at the using cell. Once you have implemented kanban, the AFT system will generate a *manufacturing traveler* initiating the build that shows where to deliver the completed item.
- Perform their own cycle counts after being trained.

6. *Keep bulk items, such as hardware used by the whole plant, in a central location.*

You can sever one manufacturing department at a time from the stockroom to permit a more controlled transformation. This process should begin as soon as possible—prior to implementing kanban. During the extended period of time required to implement kanban, you can already be receiving the full benefits of eliminating the stockroom.

You should exercise caution if you intend to maintain a stockroom while placing the components on kanban. In this scenario, the stockroom still houses the bulk of the material while the shop floor has kanban containers that run back and forth to the stockroom for replenishment. This method is even more ineffective than having a traditional stockroom employing kit pulls, for two reasons:

1. Under the traditional methodology of kit pulls, the part numbers on the pick list are arranged by stock locations, so the most effective route for the stock puller is determined and applied by the computer. When you have individual containers going to the stockroom for replenishment, the picks from one container to the next are scattered throughout the stockroom, a highly inefficient system.

2. The traditional manufacturer usually batches the build and so minimizes the number of times he or she pulls a kit. In this setup, the individual stockroom bins are visited less frequently than where smaller quantities are maintained on the floor—a situation that usually requires more frequent pulls.

Also under this method, it is fairly common to require additional stock personnel. The most effective way to use kanban is to house and deliver the material directly to the point of use. This eliminates non-value-added activities.

Deduct point identification/input. Once you lay out the assembly line/work cells and have identified the components' location, you need to enter the deduct points into the system for each bill of material.

Performance Measurement

Performance measurement is essential to gauging progress and identifying areas that need improvement. It also focuses attention on what the company deems important and motivates people to achieve the desired results. You should display these measurements in a convenient place so everyone can be aware of the progress of the shop. Measurements must be simple and based upon quantitative data. These measurements may include

- Quality levels
- Customer on-time performance
- Value-adding ratio (expressed as a percentage, value-adding time divided by total time, multiplied by 100)
- Overall equipment effectiveness
- Machine changeover time
- Supplier performance
- Through-put time
- Inventory levels
- Sales dollars per person

Container Selection

You must carefully analyze each part in determining the *container option* that will be applied and the *specific type of container* to be utilized. This

Container Options	Application
Single container	• Components too large for a container. • Supplier is at a great distance and parts are extremely inexpensive. Return cost of the container is too expensive relative to the part (full kanban lot size). • Parts are extremely expensive and setup time is not an issue—one for one. • OEM not versed in quick changeover. Full kanban lot size must be run. • Inventory must be accurate from a triggering standpoint.
Dual container	• Small components. • The supplier base is located within two days from the plant. Round trip conveyance lead time is not an issue. Low cost components. • Inventory accuracy does not impact this application from a triggering standpoint. • OEM not versed in quick changeover. Full kanban lot size must be run.
Triple container	• Application used for long distance suppliers. • Small components. • Inventory accuracy does not impact this application from a triggering standpoint.
Multiple container	• Sheer volume and size of components dictate. • Inventory accuracy does not impact this application from a triggering standpoint.

Figure 4-5. Container Option Selection

plays an important role in protecting the parts, minimizing packaging and handling costs, and facilitating the receiving process. There are three steps in selecting and preparing the proper container.

Step 1: Determine the container option that will be applied. The container options are single container, dual container, triple container, and multiple container. An option is selected based upon the specific characteristics and circumstances of the individual component (see Figure 4-5).

Step 2: Determine the specific type of container. Typically, four to five sizes of containers will suit 80% of the part numbers. The containers for the balance of the part numbers are usually custom built. The following describes how you select the specific type of container after determining the container option.

Single Container. This container option remains stationary at the point of use, where the total of on-hand plus on-order is automatically and continuously compared to the kanban lot size. When this total falls below the kanban lot size, an order is automatically triggered at the work cell or supplier responsible for replenishment. If the supplier is responsible for replenishment, he or she will use his or her standard packaging. Once you perform the receipt on the components in the receiving department, the AFT system generates a purchasing traveler indicating the point of use. The components will go directly to the point of use unless the traveler indicates that the items must be inspected first. When the components arrive at the work cell, they are placed in the container at the point of use, and the supplier packaging is then discarded.

If it is an internally made component, reusable transportation containers are used and returned. The key is the size of the container that is used at the point of use to house the components. The size of the container is predicated upon the highest average daily demand of that component that the work cell will be using. This is determined by taking the highest average daily volume of the parent part number and multiplying it times the "quantity per" of the component under consideration. The highest average daily demand of the component is then applied to the kanban lot size formula to ascertain the maximum quantity that could possibly reside at the point of use. This quantity relative to the size of the component determines the size of the container at the point of use.

The container's dimension in most cases determines the size of the work cell. The greater the inventory you carry at the point of use, the bigger the work cell. The bigger the work cell, the more inefficient the work cell. In some cases you may have to make a trade-off by having a smaller quantity of components residing at the point of use with an overflow rack located in close proximity to the work cell. Keep in mind that the smaller the quantity located at the point of use, the more frequently the operator has to stop to obtain replenishment. This type of analysis has to be performed on each component when designing work assembly cells.

Dual/triple container. You design this container option to hold a full kanban lot size. Since the kanban lot size varies, you must take into consideration the magnitude of variation. Typically, the average kanban lot size should not consume more than 50% of the container. This permits an increase of the kanban lot size of up to 100% before a problem occurs. In most cases, this container selection methodology will suffice.

Multiple container. You select this container option whenever the size and volume of the component dictates it. The ideal situation is not to force the "family of part numbers" to run together because of long setup times. Other key points include:

- Simplify the receipt process count with multiple containers since the containers hold a standard quantity of parts.
- Prevent injury by exercising care when determining the total weight of the items in the container.

Step 3: Container preparation. Several options can significantly eliminate non-value-added activities from the creation and receipt of triggered orders:

Bar-coded labels. Bar-coded labels that show the part number are permanently affixed to the dual and triple containers. When the containers are received by the receiving department, they are taken out of the egg crate and placed on a modified electronic weight scale that is hooked up to the computer system. When the bar code is scanned, the MRPII system brings up the purchase order number and determines the count in the container and compares it to the order quantity. The weight of the component and container is located in the item master file. If the count is within tolerance, the MRPII system automatically transacts the receipt. The system then generates a purchase receipt traveler indicating where the component should be delivered.

Enlarged picture of component. An enlarged picture of electronic components is permanently affixed to the dual and triple containers. The photograph is taken with a macro lens and then permanently bonded to the container. Electronic components are rich with color codes and numbers that allow a visual inspection. Once the purchase receipt traveler is generated, the container is delivered to an incoming area of the work cell. The operators visually compare the components to the picture prior to locating the container at the point of use. This process eliminates the formal inspection step.

The two options of permanently affixing bar code labels or enlarged pictures on the dual- and triple-container options are not used on the multiple containers because the containers are not permanently assigned. Instead, they are added and subtracted according to the fluctuation in average daily demand.

Supplier Performance Rating and Supplier Contracts

An important, and often overlooked, kanban prerequisite is that the OEM puts into place supplier performance measurements to assess and strengthen the supplier base—prior to implementing kanban. Supplier performance is vital to most OEMs, since a weak supplier base can significantly impact the OEM. You should automate these performance measurements; they measure the key elements of on-time delivery, full quantity ordered–full quantity received, and quality. These individual ratings are ratios expressed as a decimal and are multiplied by each other to ascertain an overall rating for each supplier (see Chapter 8).

The decision to waive inspection under the kanban system is usually made from the above rating system via a part-by-part rating. If quality becomes an issue for any given part, the inspection department can code the item master file so that the part requires inspection. Upon receipt of the part, the AFT system will generate a purchasing receipt traveler directing the part to the inspection department. You should put a formal program in place to work with low-performing suppliers. Either you can help them upgrade their capability, or you need to find a new supplier. The former is preferred to the latter in a number of cases.

Supplier contracts are essential in establishing a kanban program with the supplier base. They eliminate the non-value-added activities of negotiating pricing and delivery each time an order is placed. They also eliminate phone calls, faxes, and generating hard-copy purchase orders with its accompanying mailing cost and internal distribution. The key elements of the supplier contract include

- Pricing
- Cancellation of contracted items
- Lead-time quantity
- Supplier lead time
- Expected performance rating
- Quick changeover program
- Download capability
- Transportation considerations

Pricing. Pricing is predicated upon MRP's net projected demand for one year. You should clearly state in the supplier contract that this quantity represents an estimate, not a commitment. Also you or the supplier should have the option of renegotiating the pricing within six months if the estimated usage quantity is off by more than an agreed percentage (for example, 25%).

The supplier should also understand that if they wish to renegotiate pricing on a specific part due to lower volumes purchased than anticipated, any price change will affect only what is to be delivered, not what has been delivered. This also works the other way around if the volume being procured is higher than anticipated. The risk is mutual. In addition, if the supplier wishes to renegotiate the contract, it is understood that the OEM can solicit bids from other suppliers on the specific parts being renegotiated. If the OEM decides to buy parts from a different supplier, the OEM is still responsible for the lead time quantity of the original supplier.

Cancellation of contracted items. A number of supplier contracts permit cancellation of a contract with a written notice X days before the effective date. It is vital that the number of days specified is not less than the "longest standard lead time" to acquire the item from another source. Remember, the amount of inventory being carried at your facility is far less than the standard lead time.

Lead-time quantity. Most fabrication and machine shop suppliers still rely on *economical order quantities* to compensate for long setup times. This contributes to making their lead times excessive. In order to compensate for this condition, you must request that the supplier carry the *lead-time quantity* on their shelves until they are able to respond within a short period. This lead-time quantity is equal to the OEM's average daily demand times the supplier's total lead time to manufacture or acquire the component.

For example, if the supplier's total lead time is 20 days and the OEM's average daily demand is 100 pieces per day, you would request the supplier to carry a 2,000-piece lead-time quantity on the shelf. When the OEM triggers orders for replenishment, the quantity on the supplier's shelf will fall below the 2,000 pieces. When this occurs, the supplier will need to initiate a replenishment order within his or her facility. The supplier will also be responsible for continuously comparing his or her total of on-hand plus on-order quantities to the lead-time quantity. Once this total falls below this lead-time quantity, the supplier will launch an order to equal the lead-time quantity within his or her facility. The OEM, however, is responsible for this lead-time quantity inventory in the event of engineering changes or market place discontinuation (for OEM-unique items, not commercially available items).

In most cases the supplier does not carry any more inventory than under the traditional methodology (see Figure 4-6). For example, if the average lead time for machine components is six weeks, the buyer will at a minimum launch purchase orders to cover requirements that fall within the *time horizon* of the MRP explosion frequency plus lead time of the supplier. The order size normally equals a minimum of six weeks with split deliveries. The supplier in most cases will run all the compo-

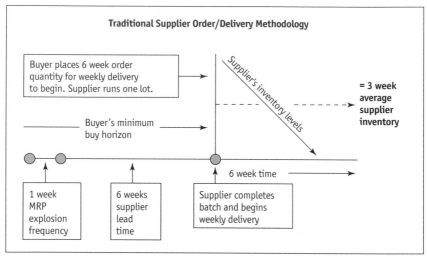

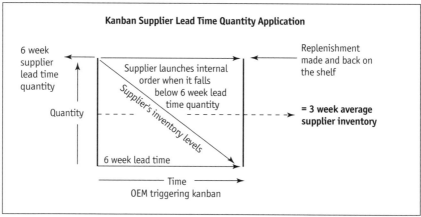

Figure 4-6. Traditional Supplier Inventory Levels versus Kanban Lead Time Levels

nents at once and deliver according to the buyer's split delivery dates. When the supplier runs a six-week quantity, his or her average inventory will equal three weeks (one half of the order quantity). Under kanban, the OEM will ask them to carry the lead-time quantity, which in this example is six weeks. When the OEM triggers an order, the supplier fills the requirement from the lead-time quantity sitting on the shelf. When the lead-time quantity falls below the six-week lead-time quantity, the supplier will launch a replenishment order within his or her facility. The average inventory in carrying the lead-time quantity would be one half the supplier's internal order quantity, which equals three weeks, the same amount of inventory as carried under the traditional methodology. The distinction is that the supplier is covered by the supplier kanban contract instead of a purchase order, and it is documented and counted upon for quick delivery.

Supplier lead time. The supplier lead time to the OEM should equal the supplier's packaging and transportation time after receipt of the downloaded purchase order. The OEM should specify in the contract the agreed upon lead time. The lead time is the same for all the part numbers carried by the supplier, regardless of the supplier's different internal lead times to manufacture or acquire. This is because they carry the lead time quantities on their shelf ready for delivery to the OEM.

Expected performance rating. The OEM should state the expected levels of performance in the contract. If the suppliers do not meet the expected performance levels, the OEM reserves the right to terminate the contract. Usually, corrective measures are worked out with the supplier to eliminate performance issues.

Quick changeover program. If the supplier setup times are an issue, the supplier must participate in a quick changeover program. The OEM should also request that they present a quarterly report reflecting their progress. This is important because the OEM is being held accountable for obsolescence due to the supplier's lead times—lead times that usually are a direct result of long setup times. It is the supplier's responsibility to lower the OEM's exposure.

Download capability. The supplier is expected to obtain download capability. As discussed above, this is fairly inexpensive. It only requires a personal computer, modem, and off-the-shelf telecommunication software. The supplier's agreement to obtain this capability should be stated in the contract.

Transportation considerations. The OEM should specify in the contract who has responsibility for transportation costs. Of special concern is the return trip of the empty containers to the supplier. The supplier should pick up the costs if there are savings from consolidation of shipment or packaging costs due to the use of containers or egg crates. If the costs are not fully absorbed through these savings, the OEM should bear responsibility for the balance. The supplier contract is an essential ingredient in relieving both the OEM and the supplier base from the daily, repetitive, non-value-added function of launching, realigning, and canceling orders.

Consolidation of supplier base. To consolidate your supplier base to an exceptional few takes a number of years to achieve. The implementation of kanban begins with the suppliers that the practitioner feels confident will be retained. The decision on which suppliers to retain is predicated upon

- Past and current performance measurements
- Overall costs
- Shop capabilities and capacity
- Financial stability
- Management stability
- Past working relationship
- How receptive suppliers are to kanban and the quick changeover program
- Distance from plant; the supplier chosen may not necessarily be the one closest to the plant

Data Integrity

Accurate perpetuation of data is essential for any automated system. Systems are only as effective as the data that they are based on. The AFT system is no exception, and requires the accurate upkeep of the following files:

- Bill of materials for accurate backflushing.
- Inventory balances and on-order information. This is used for ascertaining parts availability prior to a release to build, kanban single-container application (automatic triggering of orders based upon on-hand and on-order quantities), and kanban lot size calculation (simulation routine).
- Item master file. This file is heavily relied upon by the automated kanban system, as is demonstrated in Chapter 6 on MRPII and kanban integration.

PREREQUISITES COMPLETED

Observers of the AFT system in action are impressed with its simplicity and effectiveness. Not so obvious are the amount of forethought and implementation of prerequisites that preceded kanban to make it simple and effective. Now that you are in the process of creating a high level of performance through implementing a JIT environment, you are well on your way to establishing the prerequisites needed for an effective kanban system. As discussed at the beginning of this chapter, during the implementation of these kanban prerequisites you need to focus on the three main objectives as they relate to kanban: reducing manufacturing and supplier replenishment lead time, reducing batch sizes, and rectifying obstacles that can impede replenishment performance. Once you have achieved the three kanban objectives through the implementation of the prerequisites, you have created the kind of operational environment that kanban was intended to control. Without these prerequisites, you will have an environment that controls kanban. Another prerequisite to eliminating non-value-added activities is the integration of the kanban calculation program and cell-staffing calculation program with MRPII, which is discussed in Chapter 6. First, however, we must discuss how to implement kanban now that you have implemented the prerequisites.

Notes

1. Shingo, Shigeo. *A Revolution in Manufacturing: The SMED System.* Portland, Ore.: Productivity Press, 1985.
2. Ohno, Taiichi. *Toyota Production System: Beyond Large-scale Production.* Portland, Ore.: Productivity Press, 1988.
3. Nakajima, Seiichi. *Introduction to TPM: Total Productive Maintenance.* Portland, Ore.: Productivity Press, 1988.
4. Ibid.
5. The Productivity Press Development Team. *Quick Changeover for Operators: The SMED System—Shopfloor Series.* Portland, Ore.: Productivity Press, 1996.
6. Ibid.
7. Ibid.
8. The Productivity Press Development Team. *Mistake-Proofing for Operators: The ZQC System—Shopfloor Series.* Portland, Ore.: Productivity Press, 1997.
9. Hirano, Hiroyuki. *Poka-Yoke: Improving Product Quality by Preventing Defects.* Portland, Ore.: Productivity Press, 1988.
10. Ibid.

5

implementing kanban

Each kanban implementation is different depending upon the unique characteristics of the company. Nevertheless, some basic implementation guidelines apply to the majority of companies. In this chapter, we provide a general guideline of how to implement kanban for both the OEM's internal operation and the supplier base, and then discuss how fast you should implement kanban.

OEM INTERNAL KANBAN IMPLEMENTATION

Implementation begins at the OEM, not the supplier base, for the following two reasons:

The OEM must generate linear demand patterns for the supplier. If the OEM is still building in batches and the supplier is maintaining a lead time quantity expecting a linear demand, a stock-out will occur. For example, let's say that the OEM builds a final product item part number 5643. Part number 5643 takes a quantity of one per of part number 1234, which is furnished by a supplier. If the OEM downloads an MRP projection to the supplier indicating an average daily demand of 100 pieces per day, and the supplier's internal lead time is three days, the supplier will carry a lead time quantity of 300 pieces on the shelf. If the purchasing replenishment lead time was two days, the OEM may have two days' worth (200 pieces) of the supplier's material sitting at the point of use. If the OEM decides to batch-build 600 (six day's worth) units in one day, a stock-out will occur. Kanban requires a linear demand, and that begins with the OEM.

There is a degree of expertise that comes from implementing and running a kanban system. Before placing the suppliers on kanban, OEMs should gain that expertise by applying the kanban application to themselves before telling their suppliers how to do it. This first-hand knowledge carries a lot of weight with the suppliers, especially when they physically see how it functions on the OEM's floor. This knowledge will help the OEM in providing guidance to the supplier base.

Begin Implementing Kanban at Final Assembly

Implementing kanban at the component level before the final assembly will create stock-outs. This occurs because of reason number 1 covered above. The final assembly item must be load-smoothed and sequenced before you move on to implement the next lower level item on kanban. You can place the final assembly on kanban even though the lower levels at this point are still batched and procured by MRP. Once the final assembly item is on kanban, you can focus on implementing kanban for the next level of internally made supporting items. This approach cascades down the bill of material level by level, until you have implemented kanban at the lowest manufacturing component level. Then you will be ready to implement the suppliers one at a time.

Impact of Nonlinear Demand Patterns

Kanban is designed to operate with a linear demand pattern. MRP, on the other hand, is better suited to handle the peaks and valleys of a nonlinear demand pattern. With MRP, the inventory will rise and fall with the timing and quantity of the projected demand. If the same nonlinear demand pattern existed under a *manual* kanban, stock-outs would certainly occur since there is nothing in the calculation process that looks for nonlinear demand patterns (front loads, spike demands, or erratic demand patterns). It would be unrealistic to acquire and analyze this data by hand under manual kanban. The AFT system, however, does offer some protection against nonlinear patterns in the kanban lot size calculation/simulation process (see Chapter 7). Even with AFT's ability to capture and deal with nonlinear demand, there are still side effects with kanban. One is the carrying of high inventory levels until the highest peaks of demand are satisfied. For example, once a spike demand is visible to the AFT system—the user tells AFT how far out to go to calculate kanban lot size—it immediately adjusts the kanban lot size upward. Kanban can be triggered several times for the higher kanban lot size until the demand is encountered and satisfied. This elevates the inventory prior to the actual high demand (point of need). This differs from MRP, which times the items to come in at the high demand point of need, then lowers them to the next level of demand. Some practitioners might ask, "Why not keep the kanban lot size low prior to need and increase it just when you need it?" The answer: "Sounds like MRP, so keep it on MRP." The issue that arises with kanban is that the more nonlinear the demand patterns, the higher the inventory levels needed to accommodate them. Although not bulletproof, the AFT system will try to protect the user from this by automatically

1. Capturing front loads and spike demands
2. Adjusting the kanban lot size to avert the stock-out, notifying the user if intervention is required
3. If simulated, adjusting the kanban lot size due to erratic demand patterns to avert the stock-out

The kanban lot size will be lowered on the next explosion as long as a nonlinear demand is not present within its horizon scan (see Chapter 7 for a discussion on horizon scan). If a kanban item experiences excessive inventory, it is usually because of nonlinear demand patterns, and the mistaken selection of it as a kanban item.

Selecting Specific Part Numbers for Kanban

Not every part number can or should be on kanban. That is one reason that it is important to maintain the integrity of the MRP module as it was initially designed. A second reason is that fully implementing kanban takes an extended period of time, and there needs to be an alternative procurement method in place until that is done. Most companies can run a hybrid seamless replenishment methodology as described in this book. There will be both kanban items and MRP items. To know which part numbers should be on kanban, you must

1. Analyze the demand patterns of the item
2. Analyze the volume of the item
3. Understand the component's profile

Analyzing the demand patterns. The first step in analyzing the demand patterns is to look at the actual sales history (customer requested ship date and quantity) for the past year of the final product. How linear is it? If it is not linear, can it be made linear? With the kanban prerequisites in place, your company should be in a better position to service the customer. This includes responding to smaller order quantities without the high cost of setup times. You may be in a position to discuss ordering patterns with your main customers that can aid your company and theirs if they do not batch order. Often, customers order in batches because of the higher prices they are charged for ordering smaller quantities more frequently. If you cannot arrange this with your customers, is it possible to smooth the demand through a master production schedule by carrying some finish-goods inventory during projected low points? You may carry more finish goods with this approach at times, but there are trade-offs, such as a more efficient running facility (less overtime) and lower subassembly and component inventories as a result of a smooth demand by employing kanban. Once you have load smoothed the top-level demand patterns as much as possible, you should develop a master production schedule that reflects the improvements and explode an MRP. With these top level improvements put into place, you are now ready to study the output of MRP for the assembly/component level.

First, select the part numbers that have a fairly linear demand that are classified as A items (A, B, C classification where A items typically represent 20% of the volume of part numbers and equal 80% of the inventory dollars). Then calculate by hand the final kanban lot size for the specific kanban candidates and perform a simulation on the selected item (as demonstrated in Chapter 7). Next, determine the average inventory quantity that you would carry under kanban and determine a dollar value. Finally, compare the kanban average inventory dollars to what you are currently carrying in dollars with MRP. If the average inventory for an item under MRP is $30,000 versus an average inventory of $15,000 under kanban, kanban may be the right way to go. If, however, the running average for kanban inventory is $30,000 and MRP is at $15,000, the item may be better off on MRP. If the dollar amounts of MRP and kanban are approximately the same, you are usually better off with kanban, since you can eliminate the non-value-added activities of MRP. The rationale behind this is that, although the demand patterns may not be perfectly smooth visually, they may still be a candidate for kanban. The purpose of this analysis on A items is not to pursue inventory reduction but to use your inventory levels as a barometer to determine whether you should be using kanban or MRP. For this analysis to have merit, the MRP projection needs to be accurate. Accuracy, in this case, is defined in terms of consumption equaling MRP projection.

For B and C items (resistors, hardware, wire, for example), this step of the analysis is usually less stringent. In this case, 80% of the part numbers represents 20% of the dollars. In terms of a demand pattern, applying safety stock compensates for erratic demand items. Whether B and C items are carrying more or less inventory is usually not a major concern. What you are really after is eliminating the non-value-added activities and improving customer response time by going onto kanban. You minimize the frequency of transportation and handling costs on inexpensive components. Most of the B and C items are usually candidates for kanban as far as this phase of the analysis is concerned, but they still must pass the next two steps of the analysis.

Analyzing the volume of the item. If the volume of an item is fairly high, it may be a good candidate for kanban. If it has minor usage, it may be better suited for MRP. The rationale is straightforward: If it is a minor usage item it may not be worth the effort to place it on kanban even if the demand is linear. There is a cost associated for each part number that goes on kanban that entails the expense of containers, bar codes, and possibly pictures. An item that has minor usage is better handled by using MRP with generous lot-sizing.

Understanding the item's profile. The item should have a good quality history with minimal engineering changes. It should not be a newly introduced item with an unknown projected volume or questionable manufacturability. Anything that stands out with the item that may impact replenishment within replenishment lead time must be taken into consideration in the selection process and/or application of safety stock.

How to Handle Common Components

In designing a work cell, you should do everything possible to have only one location per part number, but sometimes this is not possible when you use the same part number in two or more work cells. The question is how to handle this situation, especially for hardware items. The basic approach utilizes a *superior container* centrally located with *subordinate containers* located at the various points of use. When the subordinate containers become empty, they are refilled at the superior container. It is the superior container that gets triggered, replenished, and delivered back to the central location.

Perform Cycle-Counting

Data integrity is key to maintaining inventory. This is especially true when employing a single-container kanban option that is totally reliant upon the accuracy of the inventory and order condition. In the realm of world class manufacturing, cycle-counting is still a very valuable tool in maintaining the integrity of the inventory records. Since the inventory is stored at the point of use (you have eliminated the stockroom) the accuracy of the inventory should rest with the operators. They are in a better position to cycle-count, since they have a more intimate knowledge of the parts than would be expected of stockroom personnel. The operators can easily flag issues and rectify problems. Inventory is usually much more accurate stored on the floor when your operators are properly trained.

Applying Safety Stock

The OEM should implement the kanban prerequisites before implementing kanban internally. In addition, the supplier base should be well accustomed to delivering what is ordered on a timely basis with the expected quality levels prior to kanban. These actions will minimize the need for large quantities of safety stock when applying kanban. As a rule, the degree to which the prerequisites have not been put into place, in conjunction with specific issues with the individual profile of the kanban item, dictates the degree to which you apply safety stock. The application of safety stock on B- and C-classified components tends to be more liberal compared to the more stringent A components. As covered in Chapter 2, when first implementing kanban, you usually apply safety stock across the board and gradually reduce it with experience.

Track the Inventory Levels

When you are selecting candidates for kanban, the demand patterns are assessed as discussed above. From this assessment, you can estimate the amount of inventory reduction for an item or a group of items selected to be placed on kanban. You usually select groups of items to go on kanban for a specific supplier or a specific work cell. From the demand pattern analysis, you may determine that the inventory for a specific group of items should go down, for example, by 65%, after being implemented on kanban. Before implementing kanban, you need to ascertain the total current inventory dollars under MRP for this specific grouping of part numbers.

Once you determine this and implement the grouping of part numbers, you need to track the inventory levels. This is accomplished by assigning the same planner code number to this specific grouping of part numbers. The MRPII system should have a routine programmed that multiplies the on-hand quantity by the standard cost, listed by planner number, to ascertain total on-hand inventory dollars for this grouping of part numbers. You need to run this report every so often by planner code to see whether the inventory is being reduced to the levels anticipated. Because of the effectiveness of kanban over the MRP methodology, what occurs in most cases is that the inventory levels will take an immediate dive and then level out.

For example, supplier items under MRP have long lead times coupled with forecasting errors. Under kanban, the suppliers carry the lead time quantities, thus drastically reducing the amount of inventory that needs to be carried at the OEM. What occurred under MRP was that the supplier was carrying inventory as well as the OEM. The supplier maintained the inventory as a result of batch runs due to long setups and delivered the items according to the purchase orders' split deliveries. The OEM's inventory built up as a result of the difference between forecasted demand versus actual demand. With kanban, there is little to no build up of inventory at the OEM from unrealistic forecasted demand. The kanban lot size can be slightly inflated, since it also uses the MRP explosion to calculate kanban lot sizes, which encompasses the inflated forecast. Its impact is usually negligible, however, due to short lead times under kanban as compared to the high levels of inventory under MRP, dealing with long lead times. What should occur if kanban is properly implemented is that the inventory carried by the suppliers stays about the same while the OEM's inventory, accumulated because of bad forecasting coupled with long lead times, decreases immediately and significantly. The reason that you track the inventory is to ensure that the kanban system is performing as anticipated (for example, estimating a 65% drop in inventory), but if your inventory levels remain stagnant or increase, you must immediately find out why. The culprit usually lies in a too generous use of minimums, multiples, and safety stock.

OEM Kanban Procedures and Training

You need to establish procedures for the kanban system and train people how to use it prior to its implementation. The procedures and training should include

- Safety stock settings
- Minimum and multiple settings (see Chapter 7)
- Kanban formula (see Chapter 7)
- Formula modifier setting (see Chapter 7)
- Triggering and receiving containers
- Specific pickup and delivery points with respective timing
- Container selection and preparation (see Chapter 4)
- Transportation considerations
- Required action if supplier's rating is below X%, etc.

Key Processes to Monitor During the OEM's
Internal Implementation

The following activities of the operators should be monitored carefully by everyone concerned during the initial phases of the OEM's internal implementation to ensure they are occurring as intended:

- Triggering the dual and triple containers as soon as they are empty; the multiple containers must be triggered as soon as consumption begins on the container.
- Placing the empty containers at the assigned pickup points as soon as they are bar scanned and then following up to ensure that the empty containers are not accidentally placed behind the full containers.
- Making sure the pickup and delivery of containers are kept on a strict schedule.
- Putting away incoming (replenishment) containers at the point of use as soon as they are delivered.

IMPLEMENTING KANBAN WITH YOUR SUPPLIER BASE

OEMs need to advise their suppliers in advance that they plan on implementing kanban with them. The more time you give them, the more time they have to begin their preparations and allow for an orderly transition to kanban. OEMs should also have a good idea from an operating standpoint of what they expect from the supplier base, so they need to discuss these basics with them. This conversation should be timed to take place 6 to 12 months before the OEM plans to begin implementation with the supplier base. Although several years may elapse before you place all the key suppliers on kanban, it is best to advise all of them up front. It is a small world, and what is told to one supplier will eventually get around to all of them.

Supplier Performance Ratings

As discussed in Chapter 4, it is imperative that the OEM put in place a supplier rating system. Without the supplier rating, the OEM has no way of knowing how good the individual suppliers are. You need to implement this rating system long before the suppliers are placed on kanban. Certain suppliers perform well in all areas, others need to improve, and some may need to be replaced.

The buyers must first make sure the rating report on supplier performance is and remains accurate. You can do this by ensuring that (1) the incoming receipts are received the same day they hit the receiving dock, and (2) agreed upon due dates and quantities are entered into the MRPII system immediately. Without this accuracy, there is no measurement; without the measurement, there is no supplier improvement.

Suppliers That Should Not Be Placed on Kanban

The main criteria for selecting suppliers were covered in Chapter 4. You should never force a supplier onto the kanban program. It is almost a sure bet that if you have to convince or prod the supplier to go on the kanban program, your relationship with him or her will deteriorate within a short time, resulting in lost effort, time, and expense. If the supplier does not care to participate, find one that does. There are many good, progressive suppliers that would be happy to receive more business.

Selecting Specific Part Numbers for Kanban

Everything discussed in the manufacturing section concerning selecting specific part numbers for kanban applies to the supplier base items. An additional element that you need to take into consideration is the internal supplier lead time of the individual item. If the supplier's internal lead time is excessive, the item may be better off on MRP. "Excessive" is defined as any item that takes beyond 16 weeks. Remember, the supplier is required to carry the lead time quantity. With lead times of 20, 30, 40, 50 weeks, there is the danger of asking the supplier to carry unrealistic inventory levels on the shelf that you are responsible for.

Supplier's Involvement in the Selection of Containers

The supplier is responsible for the quality of the items that they supply. For that to remain true under kanban, they must have a say on the type of container used to transport their items. Often it is the suppliers who come up with the best recommendations. More often than not, OEMs require only a few sizes of containers for the majority of their components, but items such as machine or fabricated components often require unique container designs to protect the components adequately.

OEM as a Resource

The OEM should never ask a supplier to do something for the OEM that they themselves would not do for their customers. Similarly, the supplier base should not be protected from the hardships that are competitively placed onto the OEM. The OEM is literally in the forefront of not only striving for their own economic well-being, but indirectly for that of their suppliers as well. In order for the OEM to compete their suppliers must be equally strong. It is for this reason that the supplier contract outlined in Chapter 4 specifies that the suppliers must reduce their setup times. This is the single biggest issue facing OEMs when dealing with the fabrication and machine shop supplier base. Much of the lead time quantity guaranteed by the OEM is a direct result of the long setup time experienced at the supplier's facility. It is therefore the supplier's responsibility to have a setup reduction program put into place at their facility and report the progress to the OEM. Because of the OEM's experience in their own facility, the OEM will be fairly well-versed at reducing setup time. They can share this expertise as a resource in helping the supplier get started on a setup reduction program of their own. Eventually the suppliers will be in a position to react to demand versus carrying the lead time quantity.

Key Processes to Monitor During the Supplier Implementation

The following activities should be monitored carefully by everyone during the initial phases of the supplier's implementation to ensure they are occurring as intended:

- Ensuring that the suppliers are carrying the lead time quantities.
- Ensuring that the downloads are being made at the prescribed time.
- Ensuring that the receiving process is organized and that the items are processed the same day.
- Checking the supplier ratings for all suppliers on an on-going basis for trends and taking corrective measures or giving positive feedback as the situation merits.
- Checking the containers-due report for delinquencies for all suppliers on an on-going basis (see Chapter 8).
- Closely watching the performance of each new supplier placed on kanban, and immediately investigating and communicating with the supplier if there are any problems.

SPEED OF OVERALL KANBAN IMPLEMENTATION

Implementing kanban is a gradual process. It takes time to select and place bar codes on the containers, coordinate with the suppliers, negotiate contracts, input data for each kanban item in the system, train the people, monitor the progress, and correct problems. The operators on the floor are usually the ones who want the implementation process to go faster, as kanban makes their jobs easier. There are fewer shortages and less shifting back and forth on what to build. Nonetheless, you should proceed at a conservative speed, especially with the suppliers, since it takes time for them to go through the learning curve. Also, you should implement no more than one supplier every two months. The first suppliers you should implement are the ones whose commodity has a very short lead time (one to three days) and with components that can be obtained anywhere, such as hardware. You can gain much experience with little concern as you go through the learning curve of operating a kanban system.

The information in this chapter and Chapter 4 provides a company with the necessary tools to begin implementing a successful kanban program. Now we are ready to integrate kanban with MRPII.

6

kanban and MRPII system integration

The automated kanban system, referred to in this text as the Automated Flow Technology™ system (AFT), incorporates two newly programmed calculation modules, MRPII and its enhancements, a simplified version of EDI, and the use of bar codes. The two separate calculation programs are programmed in-house to interface with the existing MRPII package. These two calculation programs reside in the system library—a group of programs in a computer system that is available to the user for processing. The KCSP and CSCP calculation modules integrate quite comfortably with MRPII because they use many of MRPII's standard fields. The AFT system does require the use of some additional fields. You can either utilize unused existing fields in MRPII or you may be able to create new fields depending upon your specific MRPII package. Once your management information system (MIS) department programs the two calculation modules and MRPII enhancements, your MRPII system will operate exactly as before, except it will now have the capability to calculate and perpetuate a fully automated kanban system.

AFT KEY COMPUTER FIELDS AND THEIR FUNCTIONS

The following section explains the AFT system use of existing MRPII computer fields and their respective functions in calculating and perpetuating the automated kanban system. The fields are explained from a user's perspective, enabling the reader to grasp the fundamental logic of the AFT system. Those fields that are unique to the AFT system are italicized. It should also be noted that there is no change made to the programming or information in the fields for non-kanban items. All the fields used by MRPII will be applied exactly as they were originally designed. Their application, however, will change only if the part number is coded as a kanban item. We will review the fields below from a kanban application standpoint.

Part number field. This field gives the unique identifier of raw material, components, subassembly, and finish-goods inventory.

Description field. This field gives the verbal representation of the item.

Make/buy code field. The AFT system uses the MRPII's make/buy code field to determine whether it should use the purchasing replenishment lead time or manufacturing replenishment lead time in calculating and simulating the kanban lot size.

Planner code field. In the MRPII system, companies use this field to assign their planner code numbers to all *purchase part numbers* and all *manufacturing part numbers*. It is used to separate reports according to the specific buyer or planner. Under AFT the part numbers that remain on MRP will not have their planner codes changed, but the part numbers being placed onto kanban will have their planner codes changed as described below.

Purchase part numbers. There are two categories for purchase part numbers: kanban and non-kanban. Non-kanban part numbers remain untouched. Kanban part numbers are assigned planner codes according to the specific supplier from a block of planner code numbers (e.g., 22–45) reserved for supplier kanban. For example, all part numbers on kanban with supplier X will have the same planner code number (say,

22), supplier B will have a different planner code number (say, 23) for its kanban items. This identification accomplishes the following:

- The planner code informs the AFT system how to treat the individual purchase parts from an MRP and KCSP standpoint:
  1. Non-kanban items—explode (MRP) and show on buyer's MRP reports to launch, realign, and cancel orders (no changes).
  2. Supplier kanban items—explode (MRP), calculate kanban lot sizes (KCSP), do not show on buyer's MRP reports.
  The vendor number is not used for the above as it is likely that some of the part numbers with a given supplier will not be on kanban.
- You can use the planner code number for mass-loading kanban information for a given supplier when setting up that particular supplier on kanban. An example would be mass-loading a given supplier its lead time. You can just tell the computer that a certain planner code number has a specific number of days of lead time—as opposed to inputting one by one the lead time for each part number going onto kanban with a specific supplier.
- The planner code numbers for kanban items are also used to track in-house kanban inventory levels for a given supplier. Prior to implementing kanban with a given supplier, you create a computerized report that gathers by planner code number the inventory dollars that are in-house. You will use the inventory dollar levels as a benchmark. You should run this report by planner code number frequently once kanban has been implemented to appraise the direction of inventory. If, for example, the inventory levels increase for any specific planner code, you need to check these four items:
  1. *Minimum and multiple settings:* These settings override the kanban lot size calculation. The settings may be set too high.

2. *Purchasing replenishment lead time:* This lead time is used in the calculation of the kanban lot size. If the lead time is inflated, it increases the kanban lot size needlessly and in turn increases the inventory level.

3. *Safety stock setting:* This could be set too high.

4. *Demand patterns to ensure that they are linear:* If the demand patterns swing wildly from period to period, or from explosion to explosion, the item may be better suited on MRP.

Manufacturing part numbers. There are three categories for manufacturing part numbers: non-kanban, flexible work-cell kanban, and nonflexible cell kanban. Non-kanban items remain untouched, but you assign kanban part numbers planner codes according to the individual work cell from a block of planner code numbers for flexible work cells (e.g., 46–60), and nonflexible work cells (e.g., 61–75) that are reserved for internal kanban. For example, all part numbers on kanban with flexible work cell Z will have the same planner code number (e.g., 46), all part numbers on kanban with nonflexible work cell Y will have a planner code number (e.g., 61) for all of its kanban items. This identification accomplishes the following:

- The planner code informs the AFT system how to treat the individual parts from an MRP, KCSP, and CSCP standpoint:
  1. Non-kanban item—explode (MRP) and show on planner's MRP reports to launch, realign, or cancel orders (no changes).
  2. Flexible work cell—explode (MRP), calculate average daily demand (KCSP), calculate cell staffing levels (CSCP), do not show on planner's MRP reports.
  3. Non-flexible work cell—explode (MRP), calculate kanban lot sizes (KCSP), do not show on planner's MRP reports.
- You can use the planner code number for mass-loading kanban information for a given cell when setting up that particu-

lar cell on kanban. For instance, in mass-loading the manu-facturing lead time for a given cell, you can just tell the computer that planner code number 61 has, say, a two-day lead time, instead of having to input the lead time for each of the part numbers one by one.

- The planner code number for kanban items is also used to track in-house kanban inventory levels for a given cell. Prior to implementing kanban with a given cell, you would run the same computerized report that you used for purchasing in determining current inventory levels. This is then used as a benchmark. You should run this report by planner code number frequently once you implement kanban to appraise the direction of inventory. If the inventory levels for the manu-facturing part numbers increase for any planner code, you need to check the same areas you did for purchase part num-bers: the minimum, multiple, and safety stock settings, manu-facturing replenishment lead time, and demand patterns.

Vendor number field. Under MRPII, each supplier is assigned a vendor number, which is used to identify who the supplier is for a specific part number to sort reports, among other functions. This is not altered under the AFT system; however, the AFT system uses this field to gather the appropriate triggered kanban items for download to its respective suppliers, and in gathering and preparing a one-line-per-item MRP report that is downloaded to the respective supplier for its kanban items (see Chapter 8).

Manufacturing department number field. All manufactured part numbers in the MRPII system are given a manufacturing department number. This is the department that is responsible for manufacturing the item. The AFT system uses this field for the same purpose when a kanban item is triggered. When an internally made kanban item is triggered, this manufacturing department number informs the system where the item is made so the requirement can appear at the appropriate computer terminal located in the work cell.

Minimum field. MRP uses the minimum field if a supplier requires a minimum purchase order quantity or where manufactured items have minimum run quantities due to prolonged setups. The AFT system uses this field for the same purpose but in the application of calculating kanban lot sizes for the single-container full, dual-container, and triple-container options (see Chapter 7). It ensures that the kanban lot size is no smaller than the quantity in the minimum field. In these container options, the kanban lot size equals the kanban order quantity.

Multiple field. The quantity in the multiple field represents the standard container quantity used in the multiple container application and suppliers' prepackaged quantities for the single full, dual, and triple applications. The AFT system use this field to perform the following:

1. *Determine the number of multiple containers* (see Chapter 7). The quantity in the multiple field represents the standard container quantity in the multiple-container application. Once AFT determines the preliminary kanban lot size, it is divided by and rounded up to the quantity in the multiple field. For example, if the preliminary kanban lot size equaled 9,400 pieces and the multiple was 1,000 pieces (per container), AFT would round the quantity up to 10,000 pieces, which then becomes the intermediate kanban lot size. Finally, when the 10,000 piece intermediate kanban lot size is divided by the 1,000 piece multiple, AFT would calculate a total of 10 containers. The 10,000 piece intermediate kanban lot size at this point becomes the final kanban lot size for the multiple container application.

2. *Round up the kanban order quantity to the suppliers' prepackage quantity.* The quantity in the multiple field repre-

sents the suppliers' "prepackage quantity" for the single-container full, dual-container, and triple-container options. Under these kanban container options, the kanban lot size becomes the kanban order quantity. For example, during the kanban lot size calculation process, if the preliminary kanban lot size equaled 5,800 pieces and the supplier prepackage size (multiple) is 1,000 pieces, the intermediate kanban lot size would be rounded to 6,000 pieces. When a kanban is triggered, it will be for the kanban order quantity of 6,000 pieces. The use of the multiple field in these kanban container applications is usually applied to inexpensive components. This is a situation where the cost of having the supplier (usually distributor) breaking open standard prepackage boxes and counting smaller order quantities is more than if the OEM simply carried the charges for the extra inventory.

3. *Use the multiple field to lot size MRP's net demand*. This applies to multiple-container applications. If MRP's net demand for an item is 95 and the multiple is 20 pieces per container, MRP's order policy code would lot size MRP's net demand, rounded to 100 pieces, on the planned order release line. This is important if you're sending a one-line-per-item planned order release MRP report to the supplier (see Chapter 8).

Purchasing replenishment lead-time field—Unique to the AFT. AFT uses the purchasing replenishment lead-time field to calculate kanban lot sizes and perform simulations on the newly calculated kanban lot sizes (see Chapter 7). The field expresses time as days and/or a decimal fraction of a day. The purchasing replenishment lead time is the accumulated amount of time to signal a need for replenishment and to obtain and deliver it to the point of use.

Supplier lead-time field. The supplier lead time is the contractual agreed upon time required for the supplier to deliver the goods to the user's facility once they have received the download from the OEM. The supplier's lead time is used to calculate the supplier due date once the download occurs. In the dual application it is important that you look at the timing of the empty containers—the supplier must wait for the empty container to arrive before they can fill the requirement—to ensure it does not add to the lead time. In the single-container application there are no containers in transit; in the triple-container application an empty container already resides at the supplier; in the multiple the supplier has empty unassigned containers.

Manufacturing replenishment lead-time field—Unique to the AFT. The AFT system uses the manufacturing replenishment lead-time field to calculate kanban lot sizes and perform simulations on them (see Chapter 7). This field expresses time in days and/or a decimal fraction of a day. The manufacturing replenishment lead time is the accumulated amount of time to signal a need for replenishment and to manufacture and deliver it to the point of use.

Manufacturing lead-time field. The manufacturing lead-time field represents the amount of time it takes the work cell to manufacture the kanban item. The field incorporates wait time, move time, setup time, and run time. If additional elements are involved, such as inspection, you must add them to the lead time. AFT uses the manufacturing lead time to calculate the due date (optional) of the triggered kanban.

Safety stock field. AFT uses the information in the safety stock field to calculate kanban lot sizes. It is expressed as a day or a decimal fraction of a day and is used by AFT in calculating kanban lot sizes.

Quality notes field. This field allows the quality department to put in notes pertaining to the inspection procedure or build process of the individual part number. Depending on whether it is a make or a buy item, these notes will appear on the bar-coded purchasing receipt traveler or the bar-coded manufacturing traveler.

Order policy code field. In the MRPII system, the order policy code informs MRP how to lot-size the netted demand prior to offsetting it into the planned order release line. For the kanban application, the AFT system refers to the order policy code to determine what to do with the kanban lot size after it has been calculated as well as instruct MRP how to lot size. There are four kanban application codes.

1. *Single-container discrete.* The AFT system places the calculated kanban lot size in the *order point field.* The order point system compares the combined total of on-hand and on-order to the kanban lot size that is located in this field. If this combined total falls below the kanban lot size, an order will automatically be triggered for the difference (one for one). MRP's lot sizing will be discrete.
2. *Single-container full.* The AFT system places the calculated kanban lot size in the order point field and *kanban lot size field.* The order point system compares the combined total of on-hand and on-order to the kanban lot size that is located in the order point field. If this combined total falls below the kanban lot size, an order is automatically triggered for the quantity in the kanban lot size field (full kanban lot size). The AFT will also use the quantity in the kanban lot size field to lot size MRP's netted demand.
3. *Dual/triple container.* The AFT system places the calculated kanban lot size in the kanban lot size field. When an empty container is bar scanned, the quantity in the kanban lot size field (full kanban lot size) is used as the kanban order quantity. AFT will also use the quantity in the kanban lot size field to lot size MRP's netted demand.
4. *Multiple container.* The AFT system places the calculated

number of containers in the *current number of containers field*. When the bar-coded purchase traveler or bar-coded manufacturing traveler is scanned, AFT will use the multiple field as the kanban order quantity. AFT also uses the multiple field to lot size MRP's netted demand.

The MRP explosion: two key points. First, when MRP goes through the explosion process, it halts once it has gathered all the gross requirements for a specific level (low level code has been reached). The kanban calculation/simulation program (KCSP) takes over and acquires the gross requirements and performs the kanban calculation and simulation. Once the kanban lot size has been calculated: (1) MRP will refer to the order policy code to obtain lot sizing instructions, and (2) AFT will refer to the order policy code for instructions as to where to place the calculated kanban lot sizes. Once this is done, the MRP is released to explode down to the next level. This occurs level by level until the explosion is complete.

Second, although kanban items do not appear on the production planner's or buyer's MRP report (planner codes control this) to launch, realign, and cancel orders, it is still necessary to lot-size kanban requirements on the MRP explosion. This is to ensure that the lower level items reflect in their gross requirements the upper level kanban order quantities. This is necessary in determining the lower level kanban lot size. If lot-sizing does not occur at the upper level—showing discrete usage versus full kanban lot size—it will mislead the AFT system as to the required quantity/time, and a stock-out can occur on the lower level component. This holds true regardless of whether the lower level component is a kanban or an MRP item.

Kanban lot-size field—Unique to AFT. The AFT system places the newly calculated kanban lot sizes in this field for all container options except single-container discrete and the multiple-container option. The kanban lot-size field is referred to when a single-container full, dual, or triple container is triggered to obtain the kanban order quantity. When a new kanban calculation takes place, AFT moves the old quantity in this field to the *last kanban lot-size field.*

Last kanban lot-size field—Unique to AFT. AFT uses this field to store the previous kanban lot size. The KCSP uses this field to determine the count of pieces currently residing in the dual/triple-container option (see Chapter 7).

Current number of containers field—Unique to AFT. AFT uses the current number of containers field to indicate the number of containers that are assigned to each part number. A single-container kanban option has one container, a dual-container kanban has two containers, and a triple-container kanban has two containers, since the third container resides with the supplier and is not visible to the system (you should never have three containers in-house at the same time). The number of containers for the single-, dual-, and triple-container options remains constant, but for the multiple-container option, the number of containers fluctuates for the purchased and nonflexible work cell items. When there is a change (recalculation) in the quantity of containers for the multiple-container application, AFT automatically updates the current number of containers field with the new quantity. It is through this field that AFT keeps track of the quantity of kanban containers assigned to each part number. If all the containers assigned to a part number have been triggered, the system will raise a flag for a potential stock-out (for all container options except single-container). For example, if a particular part number is assigned two containers and both of these are triggered, AFT will generate an exception message indicating a potential stock-out. This exception message is in the form of an asterisk and will appear on the *purchasing kanban due report* and *manufacturing queue screen* under the heading of "Flag" (see Chapter 8).

Quantity of containers in circulation field—Unique to AFT. AFT uses this field for the multiple-container application. It represents the number of containers presently in circulation. This quantity could be different from the newly calculated current number of container field. For example, if the current number of containers is 20 and a new calculation took place today arriving at 15 containers, there are still 20 containers in circulation at this moment. An adjustment of 5 containers needs to take place. This is further discussed in the *adjust field*.

Adjust field—Unique to AFT. This field keeps track of the number of containers that must be subtracted from what is currently in circulation. In the above example, the AFT system will try to subtract five containers from the *manufacturing queue file* (triggered orders waiting to have their bar-coded manufacturing travelers printed) or from the *purchasing hold file* (triggered orders waiting to be downloaded to the supplier), depending on whether it is a make or a buy item. If there are only two containers in the manufacturing queue file, the adjust file will eliminate the two containers from this file and the three containers that still need to be eliminated will be placed in the adjust field. The AFT system will wait until containers are triggered for this part number. Triggered orders check the adjust file first before placing triggered requirements into the manufacturing queue file or purchasing hold file. If one container is triggered, the adjust file eliminates it and brings the quantity in the adjust field to a quantity of two. It continues this process until it is brought to zero or a new recalculation of containers takes place that manipulates the quantity in the adjust field.

Once the AFT system determines the new "current number of containers," it immediately performs a simple calculation to determine what action is required by AFT to bring the "quantity of containers in circulation" in line with the "current number of containers" field quantity. This calculation automatically initiates AFT to perform the appropriate action that may include

1. Subtracting containers from the "quantity in queue/hold file" if the quantity is available.

Example: Part number 54845 is a component made in-house that had 60 containers in circulation prior to the new AFT calculation (see Figure 6-1). When the new AFT calculation took place, a quantity of 46 containers was determined. This requires the subtraction of 14 containers. There are 15 containers currently residing in the queue file waiting to have their manufacturing travelers printed before production can begin. Since we need to remove 14 containers and there are 15 containers in the queue file, AFT will automatically subtract 14 containers from the queue file. This will bring the total quantity of containers that are in circulation to 46.

2. Determining and placing a quantity in the adjust file if all the containers are not available to subtract from the "quantity in queue/hold file."

Example: Part number 56432 is a component made in-house that had 26 containers in circulation prior to the new AFT calculation. When the new AFT calculation took place, a quantity of 25 containers was determined. This requires the subtraction of 1 container. Since there are 0 containers currently residing in the queue file, AFT will have to wait until a container is triggered to remove it from circulation. It will do this by placing a quantity of 1 in the adjust file. When a container is triggered, AFT will check the adjust file prior to letting the requirement show on the manufacturing queue screen. Since there is a quantity of 1 in the adjust file, the triggered container requirement will be eliminated and will not be shown on the manufacturing queue screen. When this occurs, the quantity of containers in circulation will be adjusted to a total of 25, and the quantity in the adjust field will be brought to 0.

3. Triggering additional orders if the number of containers is to be increased.

Add/Subtract Multiple Container Logic

Part number	Description	Status just prior to new AFT calculation Current number of containers	Quantity left + in adjust file	= Quantity in circulation	Vs. New AFT calculation Current number of containers	Action required → Add/Sub	Action taken by AFT → Trigger	Information used by AFT to take action → Quantity in queue/ Hold file	Action taken by AFT → Subtract from queue/ Hold file	Action taken by AFT → New quantity in adjust file
56432	Bearing	24	2	26	25	−1	–	0	0	1
54845	Flange	60	0	60	46	−14	–	15	14	0
54761	Ring	45	4	49	55	+6	6	0	0	0
65434	Shaft	35	0	35	40	+5	5	20	0	0
74327	Rotor	25	5	30	28	−2	0	0	0	2
87564	Flange	60	10	70	75	+5	5	0	0	0

Figure 6-1. Automatically Adjusting the Number of Containers

Example: Part number 54761 (a ring) is a purchased item that that had 49 containers in circulation prior to the new AFT calculation. When the new AFT calculation took place, a quantity of 55 containers was determined. This requires the addition of 6 containers. AFT will automatically trigger 6 containers, which will go into the hold file since the ring is a purchased item (containers would go into the queue file if the part were an item made in-house). This will elevate the quantity of containers in circulation to 55.

Contract price field. This field represents the agreed upon contract price with the suppliers. The contract price is downloaded with each triggered order so that potential discrepancies in pricing can be resolved prior to the supplier invoicing the OEM.

Manufacturer's part number field. Distributors carry various manufacturers' components. These commercially available components are identified by the *manufacturer's part number field.* The OEM making the purchase often requires a specific manufacturer's component, which necessitates identifying the specific manufacturer's part number. When an order is placed using the OEM's part number, the distributor typically uses a cross-reference file to identify the manufacturer's part number. You can eliminate this step as the OEM gains the capacity to download the manufacturer's part number each time a kanban purchase order is downloaded to the distributor. Once the distributor captures the data, they can manipulate it. This way they do not have to key it into their order entry system manually.

Revision letter field. A revision letter is assigned to each OEM's drawing. When engineering changes are made to the item and the drawing is changed, so is the revision letter. Revision letters are used to communicate to the OEM's manufacturing departments or the supplier base the most current revision letter so that it can be checked against the drawing to ensure that the most recent drawing is being used. You download the revision letter to the supplier with each purchase order. The revision letter is also printed on the

- Bar-coded purchasing receipt traveler
- Bar-coded manufacturing traveler

Piece/container weight field. The AFT system uses this field to determine the number of pieces being received. The incoming container is placed on the scale and bar scanned, thereby bringing up the purchase order on the computer terminal. The number of pieces is then automatically calculated and compared to the purchase order quantity. If the quantity being received is within tolerance (for example, plus or minus 1% on B items) of what was ordered, the AFT accepts it and performs the receipt in the MRPII system, which in turn generates a bar-coded purchase receipt traveler that directs where the components should be delivered.

Inspection code field. This is a yes or no field. The default is placed on yes. If an incoming item requires inspection, this field will be coded as yes. If it does not require inspection, it is coded as no. When the bar-coded purchasing receipt traveler is generated upon a receipt, it will indicate whether or not the item must be delivered to inspection.

Floor location field. This field contains the point-of-use location for each item on the manufacturing floor. It serves two purposes:

1. The bar-coded purchasing receipt traveler is printed in the receiving department when the supplier's incoming material is received. The manufacturing floor location is printed on the bar-coded purchasing traveler when the receipt is performed. It informs the receiving department, or inspection department, where to deliver it on the manufacturing floor. If the inspection code is coded for inspection, the traveler will

indicate to deliver it to inspection first, then to the floor location.

2. The manufacturing floor location is printed on the bar-coded manufacturing traveler when it is generated at the cell responsible for replenishment. This informs the cell responsible for replenishment where to deliver the completed items.

Container size field—Unique to AFT. The AFT system uses this field to print the container size on the bar-coded manufacturing traveler for the multiple-container application. This informs the responsible work cell about the size of the container to use in providing the replenishment.

Order point field. The order point field is used by the single-container option to store the kanban lot size. The total of on-hand and on-order is continuously compared to the order point quantity. If this total falls below the order point quantity, an order is automatically triggered. The order point field is automatically updated each time the AFT system calculates a new kanban lot size.

Average daily demand field—Unique to AFT. The AFT system uses this field to house the average daily demand determined by the kanban calculation/simulation program (KCSP). Since it is identified as a flexible work cell item in the planner code, the KCSP will halt the calculation after the average daily demand has been determined and will place it in this field. The cell staffing calculation program (CSCP) uses the average daily demand to determine the cell staffing requirements.

Labor content per unit field. The labor content per unit field is the total amount of labor required to build one unit. This field covers setup time, processing labor time, and move time. The cell-staffing calculation program uses this field to determine staffing requirements.

Operator effective time per day field. This field covers the amount of time the operator is producing product. The operator effective time per day field is determined by taking the total time that the operator is on-site (usually 8$\frac{1}{2}$ hours) and subtracting lunch, breaks, and other activities such as autonomous maintenance and/or cleanup. The cell-staffing calculation program uses this field to determine staffing requirements

KEY FILES REQUIRED BY THE AFT SYSTEM

MRPII is programmed to create three distinct files, each designed for a specific purpose:

1. *Supplier purchase order download file.* The following fields are gathered into a file and downloaded to the supplier for each part number that is triggered. Only the due date is calculated at the time of the download.
   - Purchase order number (automatically assigned by the system)
   - OEM's part number
   - Description
   - Manufacturer's part number (if applicable)
   - Revision letter (if applicable)
   - Quantity ordered
   - Contract price
   - Due date

   The due date is calculated at the time of download by using the supplier lead time. The OEM places the supplier on a strict schedule for performing the download of purchase orders. If this is not performed in a timely manner, a stock-out may occur. The system needs to create an exception message if a download did not occur as scheduled.

2. *Bar-coded purchasing receipt traveler file.* The bar-coded purchasing receipt traveler is printed in the receiving department when the incoming material from the supplier is accepted. This file encompasses the following fields:
   - Purchase order number

- Supplier name
- OEM's part number
- Description
- Quantity ordered
- Quantity received
- Due date
- Date/time received
- Revision number (if applicable)
- Routing (inspection and/or floor location)
- Inspection notes (if applicable)

The bar-coded purchasing traveler accompanies the components to the point of use. It is also used to trigger the multiple-container application (see Figures 3-4 and 3-9).

3. *Bar-coded manufacturing traveler file.* The bar-coded manu-
   facturing traveler is printed in the cell responsible for replen-
   ishment when the operators are ready to run the triggered
   requirement. This file encompasses the following fields:
   - Part number
   - Description
   - Quantity
   - Due date/time
   - Revision letter
   - Container option. This indicates whether the container is a
     single, dual, or multiple. In the multiple-container applica-
     tion, the total number of containers is reflected as well as
     the number of containers that are triggered.
   - Container size
   - Floor location
   - The date and time the container was triggered
   - Quality notes

   The bar-coded manufacturing traveler is generated when the
   operator is ready to produce the components. Most MRPII

systems already have the capability to perform a *parts availability simulation* in determining shortages. The parts availability simulation should be tied into the manufacturing queue file—where triggered kanban orders reside—to determine the availability of components prior to printing the bar-coded manufacturing traveler. The floor locations for the simulation should only be for the point of use at the cell, in case you use the component elsewhere in the facility. The operator's manufacturing queue screen should reflect parts availability so that an informed decision can be made prior to generating the traveler (see Chapter 8). If shortages are expected, AFT generates an exception report. The bar-coded manufacturing traveler accompanies the components to the point of use and is also used to trigger the multiple-container application (see Figures 3-7 and 3-8).

Simplified Version of EDI

The AFT system also requires a simplified version of EDI. A number of inexpensive, off-the-shelf telecommunication programs can be used to transmit files: specifically, purchase orders and a one-line-per-part-item MRP. It takes little effort and time to set up the suppliers on this methodology. All they need is a personal computer, modem, and telecommunication program. The OEM will give the suppliers a password permitting them to dial in and access their files.

The OEM must survey their supplier base before selecting a methodology. The larger suppliers usually have EDI, whereas many of the smaller suppliers do not. This simplified version of the EDI method works well for smaller suppliers, since they usually do not have an MIS staff. The larger suppliers can still use a PC to obtain their files and upload it to their main system. If the majority of the supplier base has EDI capability, the OEM may use this as opposed to the simplified version.

BEFORE PROGRAMMING THE AFT SYSTEM

There are a number of different ways to program kanban capabilities into the current package. The method you end up choosing is typically dependent upon the degree of capabilities desired and the unique characteristics of the current package and manufacturing/supplier environment. Before programming your AFT system, you should do the following:

1. Design the AFT program completely for the whole kanban system. Include the MIS, manufacturing, materials, and purchasing departments from the beginning and make sure they agree upon the final design. Programming your AFT system a piece at a time without full agreement from these departments could result in reprogramming.
2. Select a sample size of part numbers that you can calculate and perpetuate by hand. Emulate your automated design manually before programming your AFT system.
3. Once you have programmed your AFT system, run a sample quantity of part numbers to ensure that it is performing as desired. Make sure you keep high levels of safety stock when beginning implementation. Then gradually reduce it with experience.

7

AFT calculations for determining kanban lot sizes and staffing levels

anually calculating kanban lot sizes is a grueling, time-consuming task. Unfortunately, just like order point, it does not take place as often as it should. In recalculating, the chance for error is ever-present, and the time to investigate beyond the application of the basic formula for front loads, spike demands, or erratic demand patterns is often unavailable. This is particularly true when there are hundreds or thousands of components that have experienced a shift in projected demand and therefore require recalculation. The repercussion of not knowing the demand patterns boils down to a lost opportunity of averting a potential stock-out. The longer the replenishment lead time, the more severe the impact of a stock-out because of the required recovery time.

Convincing anyone to automate the processes described in this chapter takes very little effort if they've ever had to calculate kanban lot sizes by hand, calculate staffing requirements by hand, experience the impact of nonlinear demands, and/or experience the impact of not having the time to recalculate the kanban lot size. This chapter discusses the main elements and calculations that the AFT system employs in determining kanban lot sizes and staffing levels for flexible work cells.

DETERMINING KANBAN LOT SIZES WITH AFT

The AFT system is designed to perform the following functions:

1. Automatically recalculate kanban lot sizes.
2. Employ a horizon scan feature, a routine within the kanban lot-size calculation process that automatically adjusts the kanban lot size for front loads and/or spike demands.
3. Utilize a simulation routine to further test the newly calculated kanban lot sizes against the demand patterns. This feature is designed for environments that cannot respond immediately to an erratic demand pattern.

The AFT system is not designed to perform these functions:

1. Use a horizon scan or simulation routine on replenishment lead times that are expressed as a decimal fraction of a day. The complexity of the programming would outweigh the benefits gained. This is typically not an issue, because the AFT will still automatically calculate kanban lot sizes and most environments deal with replenishment lead times expressed in full days.
2. Perform a simulation on multiple-container applications. Again, the complexity of the programming would outweigh the benefits gained in an environment with immediate response capability. This, too, is not an issue, as the kanban lot sizes and number of containers will still be automatically calculated by employing the horizon scan looking for front loads or spike demands.

Gross Requirements

AFT uses gross requirements to calculate kanban lot sizes instead of net requirements. This is to safeguard against inaccurate on-hand balances and unexpected demand. If there is sufficient inventory on hand to cover the gross requirements, AFT will still calculate a kanban lot size and place it in the appropriate fields. There is no impact on inventory, since kanban should not be triggered. If the on-hand balance is actually below what was thought to be available or actual demand exceeded projected requirements, however, a kanban lot size would be ready to accommodate a kanban that is triggered.

Kanban Lot-Size Formula

The following equation reflects the kanban lot-size formula used by the AFT system.

$$\text{Kanban lot size} = (\text{ADD}) \left(\begin{array}{l} \text{Replenishment LT} \\ \text{days or decimal fraction} \\ \text{of a day} \end{array} + \begin{array}{l} \text{Safety stock} \\ \text{days or decimal fraction} \\ \text{of a day} \end{array} \right)$$

Formula Modifier

The *formula modifier* informs the kanban calculation/simulation program (KCSP) how far out in time to go to calculate the average daily demand and how far the *horizon scan* should look for front loads and spike demands. The user inputs this one setting before the MRP explosion. We describe the function of the formula modifier below by examining the average daily demand and horizon scan.

Average daily demand (ADD). If you set the formula modifier for 20 days, the KCSP will go out 20 days and obtain all the gross requirements within that span of time. It would then add the gross requirements and divide it by the number of days it went out (20 days) to arrive at the ADD. This one setting applies to all part numbers that have a planner code identifying it as a flexible work-cell kanban, supplier kanban, or nonflexible work-cell kanban. It should be pointed out that once the average daily demand is calculated for the "flexible work-cell kanban" items, its calculation will end and the average daily demand will be placed in the item master's average daily demand field. The balance of the kanban items will continue with the calculation process. (See Figure 7-1, AFT Calculation Flowchart.)

Horizon scan. The horizon scan is a routine in the kanban lot-size calculation. Its sole purpose is to guard against front loads and spike demands. Once the ADD has been determined, it is automatically multiplied by the total of replenishment lead time and safety stock to equal what is called a sub-preliminary kanban lot size. If you set the formula modifier at 20 days, the horizon scan also looks 20 days into the future for any single gross requirement that exceeds the sub-preliminary kanban lot size. If the horizon scan finds a gross requirement (front load or spike demand) that exceeds the sub-preliminary kanban lot size, it will adopt the gross requirement as the preliminary kanban lot size. If it does not locate a front load or spike demand, it will adopt the sub-preliminary kanban lot size as the preliminary kanban lot size. We discuss each step of the calculation in the next section. How far forward you should set the formula modifier is covered in this chapter.

Kanban Lot-Size Calculation Steps

The KCSP goes through the following four steps to determine the kanban lot size for all container options:

1. ADD
2. Sub-preliminary kanban lot size
3. Preliminary kanban lot size
4. Intermediate kanban lot size

The intermediate kanban lot size then goes through the simulation routine (discussed later in this chapter) for all container options except the multiple. Once it passes the simulation, it becomes the final kanban lot size. The four-step calculation process is demonstrated below for a hypothetical part number 5679 with the following characteristics:

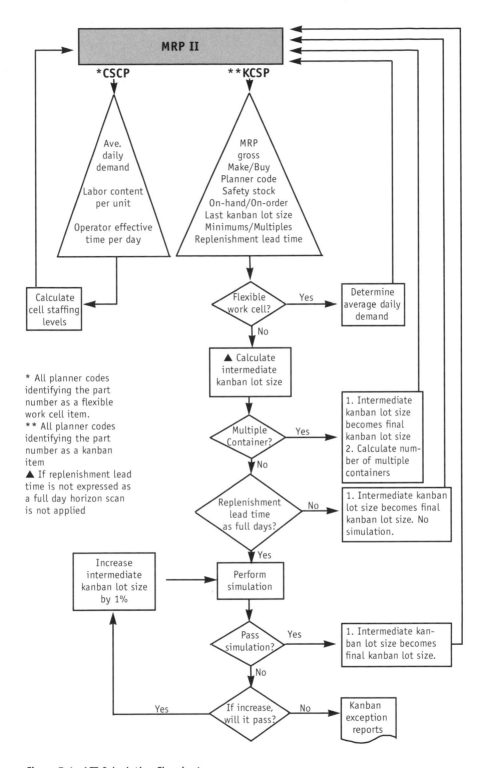

Figure 7-1. AFT Calculation Flowchart

- 2 day purchasing replenishment lead time (1 day longest download frequency + 1 day supplier lead time)
- 1 day safety stock setting
- 20 day formula modifier setting
- 0 minimum/0 multiple

Step 1: Average daily demand. The KCSP will go out 20 days and obtain the gross requirements. It will then add the 20 days' worth of gross requirements and divide the number by 20 days to determine the ADD (see Figure 7-2). The gross requirements for 20 days equal 1,600 pieces. When KCSP divides this by 20 days, it obtains an ADD of 80 pieces per day.

Part number—5679		Formula modifier—20 days
	Average Daily Demand	
Day	*MRP gross*	
1	85	
2	90	
3	75	
4	88	
5	72	
6	78	
7	80	
8	85	
9	79	
10	69	
11	70	
12	75	
13	78	
14	85	
15	90	
16	84	
17	87	
18	80	
19	70	
20	80	
	Total: 1600	

Step 1: 1600/20 = 80 average daily demand

Figure 7-2. Step 1: Calculate Average Daily Demand

Step 2: Sub-preliminary kanban lot size. The KCSP then multiplies the 80 piece ADD (per the formula) by the total of the two day purchasing replenishment lead time plus one day safety stock. Both of these are expressed in days and/or a decimal fraction of a day (see Figure 7-3). This total of three days is then multiplied by the 80-piece ADD. This equals a sub-preliminary kanban lot size of 240 pieces.

Step 3: Preliminary kanban lot size. Since the formula is set to go out 20 days on all kanban items, the horizon scan will also go out 20 days. Its objective is to search for any single gross requirement that may exceed the sub-preliminary kanban lot size. If this condition exists, the

---

Part number—5679   Formula modifier—20 days
PRLT = 2 days   Safety stock = 1 day

Sub-preliminary Kanban Lot Size

Day	MRP gross
1	85
2	90
3	75
4	88
5	72
6	78
7	80
8	85
9	79
10	69
11	70
12	75
13	78
14	85
15	90
16	84
17	87
18	80
19	70
20	80

Total: 1600

Step 1: 1600/20 = 80 average daily demand
Step 2: (80 ADD) (2 days PRLT + 1 Day SS) = 240 sub-preliminary kanban lot size

Figure 7-3. Step 2: Calculate the Sub-preliminary Kanban Lot Size

Part number—5679   Formula modifier—20 days
PRLT = 2 days   Safety stock = 1 day

Preliminary Kanban Lot Size

Day	MRP gross	Horizon scan
1	85	No
2	90	No
3	75	No
4	88	No
5	72	No
6	78	No
7	80	No
8	85	No
9	79	No
10	69	No
11	70	No
12	75	No
13	78	No
14	85	No
15	90	No
16	84	No
17	87	No
18	80	No
19	70	No
20	80	No
	Total: 1600	

Step 1: 1600/20 = 80 average daily demand
Step 2: (80 ADD) (2 days PRLT + 1 day SS) = 240 sub-preliminary kanban lot size
Step 3: No daily demand exceeds 240; 240 becomes the preliminary kanban lot size

Figure 7-4. Step 3: Calculate the Preliminary Kanban Lot Size

horizon scan adopts that specific gross requirement quantity as the *pre-liminary kanban lot size*. If this condition does not exist, it accepts the sub-preliminary kanban lot size as the preliminary kanban lot size. In continuing with this example, no single gross requirement exceeds the sub-preliminary kanban lot size. Therefore, the preliminary kanban lot size is 240 pieces (see Figure 7-4).

Figure 7-5 demonstrates the horizon scan capturing and adopting a spike demand as the preliminary kanban lot size. In this case, the sub-preliminary kanban lot size equals 282. Since there is a spike demand of 355 pieces, the system will adopt 355 pieces as the preliminary kanban

Part number—5679   Formula modifier—20 days
PRLT = 2 days   Safety stock = 1 day

Gross Requirement
Accepted as Preliminary Kanban Lot Size

Day	MRP gross	Horizon scan
1	85	No
2	90	No
3	355	**Yes—accept 355**
4	88	No
5	72	No
6	78	No
7	80	No
8	85	No
9	79	No
10	69	No
11	70	No
12	75	No
13	78	No
14	85	No
15	90	No
16	84	No
17	87	No
18	80	No
19	70	No
20	80	No

Total: 1880

Step 1: 1880/20 = 94 average daily demand
Step 2: (94 ADD) (2 days PRLT + 1 day SS) = 282 sub-preliminary kanban lot size
Step 3: 355 exceeds 282 . . . . . 355 = Preliminary kanban lot size

Figure 7-5. Demonstration of Step 3: Horizon Scan Adopts Spike Demand

lot size. For the balance of the example, we continue with Figure 7-4, which has a preliminary kanban lot size of 240 pieces. Again, you do not employ this horizon scan step for replenishment lead times expressed as a decimal fraction of a day. For items expressed as a decimal fraction of a day, the KCSP will automatically proceed to the next step.

Step 4: Intermediate kanban lot size. The KCSP applies minimum and multiple field quantities in the determination of the intermediate kanban lot size. (See Chapter 6, "Minimum Field" and "Multiple Fields" for a discussion.) If you set the minimum at 300 pieces, it elevates the preliminary kanban lot size from 240 pieces to an intermediate kanban lot size of 300 pieces. If you set the multiple at 50 pieces, you elevate the 240 piece preliminary kanban lot size to an intermediate lot size of 250 pieces. Two points need to be made regarding this:

1. The kanban lot-size calculation for a multiple-container would end here. The intermediate kanban lot size would automatically become the final kanban lot size by dividing the 250 pieces by the container capacity of 50 pieces to ascertain the number of containers, which is 5. AFT would then place the 5 containers in the *current number of containers field*. The AFT system would then automatically adjust the number of containers (see Chapter 6, Figure 6-1). Multiple containers do not go through the simulation.

2. For kanban items with replenishment lead times of less than a day, the kanban lot-size calculation would conclude at this point. Lead times of less than a day are not simulated by AFT. The intermediate kanban lot size becomes the final kanban lot size as it is transferred to the appropriate fields.

Since there are no quantities in the minimums or multiples fields for this part number, the 240 piece preliminary kanban lot size becomes the intermediate kanban lot size of 240 pieces (see Figure 7-6). Once KCSP calculates the intermediate kanban lot size, it runs a simulation routine to test it. If it passes the simulation test, the intermediate kanban lot size will become the final kanban lot size.

KCSP Simulation Routine

The KCSP simulation routine is designed to guard against erratic demand patterns. It differs from the horizon scan in that it is more thorough. It is possible to have a number of medium-sized hits in a row that are smaller than the intermediate kanban lot size and thus able to create a stock-out. If you load smooth, however, and sequence the top-level requirements,

Part number—5679		Formula modifier—20 days
PRLT = 2 days		Safety stock = 1 day

Intermediate Kanban Lot Size

Day	MRP gross	Horizon scan
1	85	No
2	90	No
3	75	No
4	88	No
5	72	No
6	78	No
7	80	No
8	85	No
9	79	No
10	69	No
11	70	No
12	75	No
13	78	No
14	85	No
15	90	No
16	84	No
17	87	No
18	80	No
19	70	No
20	80	No
	Total: 1600	

Step 1: 1600/20 = 80 average daily demand
Step 2: (80 ADD) (2 days PRLT + 1 day SS) = 240 sub-preliminary kanban lot size
Step 3: No daily demand exceeds 240; 240 becomes the preliminary kanban lot size
Step 4: 0 minimums— 0 multiples— intermediate kanban lot size = 240 pieces
*Note: If the minimum was set at 245 pieces, the intermediate kanban lot size would be 245.
    If the multiple was set at 50 pieces, the intermediate kanban lot size would be 250.

Figure 7-6. Step 4: Determining the Intermediate Kanban Lot Size

you have less of a need to perform a simulation. In addition, if the replenishment lead times of the manufacturer and suppliers are expressed as decimal fractions of a day, as opposed to numbers of days, you are capable of mobilizing a quick reaction against an imperfect demand pattern. The quick reaction capability of the manufacturer and supplier base greatly minimizes the potential impact of a less than perfect demand pattern. This capability is gained from thoroughly implementing the kanban prerequisites.

Unfortunately, most manufacturers and their suppliers do not fit this perfect profile. Their demand patterns are not perfectly smooth, and their replenishment lead times are expressed in full days, not decimal fractions of a day. They have to adjust the calculated kanban lot size according to the degree to which the projected demand pattern is nonlinear. Manufacturers require MRP's visibility, so they have time to respond to projected changes in demand. This comes by coupling KCSP with MRP, which means the adjustment to intermediate kanban lot size due to the nonlinear demand can automatically take place through the simulation routine. The simulation adjusts the kanban lot sizes accordingly and raises a flag on a computerized report (see Chapter 8) if user intervention is required. There is a threshold, however, where the demand patterns are so erratic that the item may be better off on MRP than on kanban (see Chapter 5). Although this simulation feature is designed to protect the user from erratic demand patterns, keeping the inventory levels for an item too high under kanban may mean the item is better suited for MRP.

If the simulation routine option is elected, it will run after the intermediate kanban lot size has been determined. It will test the intermediate kanban lot size to ensure that a stock-out condition will not occur against the projected demand. In effect, it emulates what should occur on the floor by comparing each container against the gross requirements in terms of

- Intermediate kanban lot size
- Current on-hand condition
- Current on-order condition
- Replenishment lead time

The simulation routine will then do one of the following three things:

1. Pass the intermediate kanban lot size (becomes the final kanban lot size) and refer it to the order policy code to determine appropriate placement (see Chapter 6, "Order Policy Code Field").

2. Fail the intermediate kanban lot size due to a stock-out—
   unsatisfied demand with zero on hand. The simulation will
   then automatically adjust the intermediate kanban lot size
   upward by 1% and run it through the simulation again,
   repeating this process until it passes. Once it passes, it will
   become a final kanban lot size and refer to the order policy
   code to determine appropriate placement (see Chapter 6,
   "Order Policy Code Field").
3. Place the intermediate kanban lot size on an exception report
   because it recognizes that it is dealing with a front load that
   requires user intervention.

Still using our example of an intermediate kanban lot size of 240
pieces, we now demonstrate a simulation for each container option: the
single-container discrete, single-container full, and dual/triple container.

Single-container full simulation. If a component's order policy code
informs the simulation routine that the component is a single-container
full application, it will use the simulation calculation format in Figure
7-7. Since the kanban lot-size calculation went out 20 days, the simulation routine goes out an equal distance. Next to each day are the associated MRP gross requirements for that particular day. These are the same
gross requirements that were used in calculating the intermediate kanban
lot size. What is labeled as KB1 (kanban container 1) is the single container residing at the point of use. The quantity under KB1 is the quantity remaining in the container after the on-hand has been applied to the
gross requirement in addition to any kanban receipts that may have
taken place. The simulation begins with the actual on-hand of 245 pieces
that exists at the time of the simulation. Next to KB1 is *kanban triggered*.
When the total of on-hand plus on-order quantities falls below the newly
calculated intermediate kanban lot size of 240 pieces, a kanban is simulated to trigger. The order quantity triggered will be equal to the newly
calculated intermediate kanban lot size. The next column is *kanban*

received. Triggered orders are received based on when KCSP launches the order in conjunction with the stated replenishment lead time. The quantity received is added to the KB1 quantity. If the kanban order was already open prior to the simulation, the simulation lists it under the kanban received column on the date it is due in. Figure 7-7 shows that the intermediate kanban lot size of 240 pieces passes the simulation. It will be accepted as the final kanban lot size and will refer to the order policy code to determine appropriate placement (see Chapter 6, "Order Policy Code Field").

This simulation emulates what should occur to the single-container full option on the floor. If the container fails this simulation with a stock-out (zero quantity on hand with an unsatisfied demand), the AFT

Part number—5679				Total on hand = 245
PRLT = 2 days				Intermediate kanban lot size = 240
		Single Container Full Option		
Day	*MRP gross*	*KB1*	*Kanban triggered*	*Kanban received*
1	85	160	240	–
2	90	70	–	–
3	75	235	240	240
4	88	147	–	–
5	72	315	–	240
6	78	237	240	–
7	80	157	–	–
8	85	312	–	240
9	79	233	240	–
10	69	164	–	–
11	70	334	–	240
12	75	259	–	–
13	78	181	240	–
14	85	96	–	–
15	90	246	–	240
16	84	162	240	–
17	87	75	–	–
18	80	235	240	240
19	70	165	–	–
20	80	325	–	240

4108/20 = 205 average inventory

240 passed the simulation; 240 = Final kanban lot size

Figure 7-7. Simulation Format for Single Container Full Application

system elevates the intermediate kanban lot size by 1% and again reruns the simulation routine. AFT continues to repeat this process until the adjusted intermediate kanban lot size passes the simulation. Once the adjusted intermediate kanban lot size passes the simulation, it becomes the final kanban lot size and will refer to the order policy code to determine where to place it. If the simulation routine stocks out because of a front load (stock-outs within replenishment lead time), it does not rerun the simulation for that part number. Instead, it will place the part number on an exception report for user intervention (see Chapter 8).

Of course there are situations in which a component requires many containers due to sheer volume. If these containers are placed on kanban and must be run in batches because of concerns about setup time, you should consider coding and controlling them as a single-container full option. In this option you handle the parts as you would manually handle them by running them as one lot on the floor. In addition, they will be able to have their kanban lot sizes tested through the single-container full simulation.

Single-container discrete simulation. The single-container discrete simulation calculation format is identical to the single-container full simulation except when KCSP launches a kanban order quantity during the simulation. It is equal to the difference between the total of on-hand and on-order as compared to the intermediate kanban lot size quantity of 240 pieces (see Figure 7-8). Once the intermediate kanban lot size of 240 pieces is accepted by the simulation, it will be accepted as the final kanban lot size and referred to the order policy code to determine appropriate placement (see Chapter 6, "Order Policy Code Field").

Of further interest is the average inventory of 84 pieces under this container option as opposed to the 205-piece average inventory of the single-container full option. Both container options operate under identical circumstances except when launching the kanban order quantity. This order quantity makes a difference. You use the single-container full application when there are concerns about setup times, and the single-

Part number—5679
PRLT = 2 days

Total on hand = 245
Intermediate kanban lot size = 240

Single Container Discrete Option

Day	MRP gross	KB1	Kanban triggered	Kanban received
1	85	160	80	–
2	90	70	90	–
3	75	75	75	80
4	88	77	88	90
5	72	80	72	75
6	78	90	78	88
7	80	82	80	72
8	85	75	85	78
9	79	76	79	80
10	69	92	69	85
11	70	101	70	79
12	75	95	75	69
13	78	87	78	70
14	85	77	85	75
15	90	65	90	78
16	84	66	84	85
17	87	69	87	90
18	80	73	80	84
19	70	90	70	87
20	80	90	80	80

1690/20 = 84 average inventory

240 passed the simulation; 240 = Final kanban lot size

Figure 7-8. Simulation Format for Single Container Discrete Application

container discrete when setup time is not an issue. What reduces inventory is the successful application of the kanban prerequisites.

Dual/triple-container simulation. Before the simulation, the KCSP makes a determination of the quantity of components residing in each container. It calculates this by retrieving the last kanban lot size and the current on-hand quantity (see Figure 7-9). If the last kanban lot size was 200 pieces and there are 245 pieces on hand, there would be 45 pieces in the front container and 200 pieces in the back container. In determining the quantity in each container, the back container is always the first to receive the on-hand inventory until it reaches the old kanban lot size (it

		Dual/Triple Application			
Example	Final kanban lot size	Current on hand	In front kanban #1	In back kanban #2	Triggered on order
1	200	245	45	200	0
2	200	260	60	200	0
3	200	300	100	200	0
4	200	90	0	90	200 due day 1

Figure 7-9. Simulation Routine Determining the Quantity in Each Container Prior to Simulation

cannot exceed the old kanban lot size). Any residual inventory is given to the front container. This is exactly how it works on the floor. You place new containers coming in with replenishment behind the container that is already present. We will use Example 1 in Figure 7-9 to demonstrate the dual/triple-container simulation. In this example there are 45 pieces in the front container (KB1) and 200 pieces in the back container (KB2).

The simulation begins by applying the first kanban container (KB1) of 45 pieces against the 85-piece MRP gross requirement (see Figure 7-10). It falls 40 pieces short of satisfying the demand. This causes KB1 to be triggered, moving KB2 forward for continued use. Now 40 pieces from KB2 are applied to the MRP gross requirement. This fully satisfies the demand, leaving 160 pieces in the container. KB2 then is applied to the second day of MRP gross requirement, which satisfies the demand and leaves 70 pieces in the container. The 70 pieces are then applied to the day-3 MRP gross requirement, and KB2 is triggered, since it is now empty. Day 3 is short 5 pieces. This shortfall is covered by KB1 arriving (within the purchasing replenishment lead time of 2 days) with replenishment equaling the new kanban lot size of 240 pieces. This leaves 235 in KB1 ready to apply to the next day's requirements. AFT continues this process all the way down through the twentieth day. If it passes the simulation, the intermediate kanban lot size of 240 pieces is adopted as the final kanban lot size. Once this occurs, the AFT system will refer to the

Part number—5679				Intermediate kanban lot size = 240	
PRLT = 2 days				Starting balance KB1 = 45	
				Starting balance KB2 = 200	
			Dual/Triple Container		
Day	MRP gross	KB1	KB2	Kanban triggered	Kanban received
1	85	0	160	240	–
2	90	0	70	–	–
3	75	235	0	240	240
4	88	147	0	–	–
5	72	75	240	–	240
6	78	0	237	240	–
7	80	0	157	–	–
8	85	240	72	–	240
9	79	233	0	240	–
10	69	164	0	–	–
11	70	94	240	–	240
12	75	19	240	–	–
13	78	0	181	240	–
14	85	0	96	–	–
15	90	240	6	–	240
16	84	162	0	240	–
17	87	75	0	–	–
18	80	0	235	240	240
19	70	0	165	–	–
20	80	240	85	–	240

1924   +   2184 = 4108/20 = 205 average inventory

240 passed the simulation; 240 = Final kanban lot size

Figure 7-10. Simulation Format for Dual/Triple Application

order policy code to determine appropriate placement (see Chapter 6, "Order Policy Code Field").

Just like the single-container full simulation, this simulation emulates what should occur to the dual/triple container on the floor. If the container fails this simulation with a stock-out (zero quantity on hand with an unsatisfied demand), KCSP will elevate the intermediate kanban lot size by 1% and the simulation routine commences once again as long as the stock-out did not occur within the replenishment lead time. KCSP repeats this process until the intermediate kanban lot size is adequate to avert the stock-out demonstrated by passing the simulation. Once it passes, this quantity becomes the final kanban lot size. If the simulation routine stocks out due to a front load, it will not rerun the simulation for that part number. Instead, it places the part number on an exception report for user intervention (see Chapter 8).

Again, of interest is the dual/triple-container average inventory of 205 pieces. This average inventory is identical to the single-container full application. This occurs because both container applications have the same full kanban lot size quantity being triggered. The kanban order quantity does influence the average inventory that is carried.

Formula Modifier Setting

The formula modifier setting informs KCSP how far out in time to go so it can

1. Gather the gross requirements to calculate the ADD.
2. Look for front loads and spike demands and adopt the front load or spike demand as the preliminary kanban lot size.
3. Perform the simulation.

If you set the formula modifier further out than it should be, the calculations can easily adopt spike demands far into the future, thus unnecessarily raising inventory on certain items prematurely. If the setting is not placed to go out far enough, however, valuable reaction time may be lost. This is because the system only responds to what is within the formula modifier setting. In other words, the spike demand may not elicit a reaction until it is within the replenishment lead time, thus causing a needless potential stock-out. In either case, the formula modifier must be set to extend into the appropriate future. The proper setting is the sum total of MRP explosion frequency, plus two times the longest replenishment lead time, as shown in Figure 7-11. The logic behind this combination of elements is this: *When a kanban lot size is calculated on day 1 and potentially triggered just before the new MRP explosion on day 5, it takes 7 days before it is received at the point of use. The quantities coming in are meant to cover a 7-day period.*

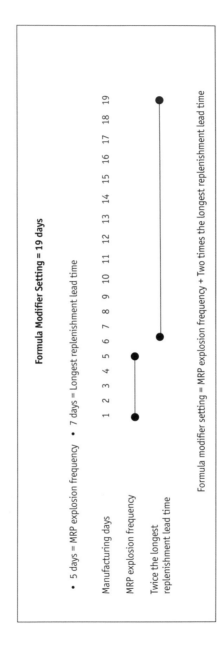

Figure 7-11. Formula Modifier Setting

DETERMINING FLEXIBLE WORK-CELL STAFFING LEVELS BY USING CSCP

Flexible work cells are usually superior in performance then nonflexible work cells or traditional manufacturing arrangements. These flexible cells usually have little to no problems with setup time and have a highly trained, multiskilled staff of operators. They are able to run a true multiple-container option, since they can produce without batching.

To calculate flexible work-cell staffing levels, the following data need to be available for each flexible work-cell number:

1. ADD
2. Labor content per unit
3. Operator effective time per day

Since the labor content per unit and operator effective time per day are fairly static, they are infrequently modified. The ADD, however, is dynamic and may change each time average daily demand is recalculated. The ADD is determined by the KCSP system in the first step of the kanban lot-size calculation routine. After KCSP ascertains the ADD, it places it in the ADD field in the item master file. The labor content per unit is usually drawn from the router file while the operator effective time per day is obtained from the work center master file. Once KCSP calculates all the kanban lot sizes, the cell staffing calculation program obtains the three pieces of data and calculates the cell staffing levels. This was demonstrated in Chapter 2. In actual application, there is often more than just one part number produced in a given cell with different labor contents and different ADDs.

To determine the flexible work-cell staffing levels for the above scenario, you should program the CSCP system to perform the following three steps for each individual flexible work cell.

1. For each component, obtain the ADD and its respective labor content per unit.

2. For each component, multiply the ADD by its respective labor content per unit

3. Add the extended totals and divide by the operator effective time. This determines the staffing levels for the individual flexible work cells.

The flexible work-cell staffing report will show the required staffing levels for each cell (see Chapter 8). The bottom of the report will show the sum total of operators required for all the flexible work cells.

The concept of a simplified manual kanban system running by itself is not impossible. It just is not applicable to a large number of manufacturers because of the sheer volume of part numbers and the constant changes in demand. In the next chapter, we explore how manufacturers can perpetuate an automated kanban system.

8

perpetuation of the automated kanban system

Many companies have invested heavily in acquiring and implementing MRPII capability. Investment comprises the costs of buying the software package, developing the procedures, and training the organization as a whole. MRP is a great planning tool but a poor execution tool, as demonstrated by its inability to respond to actual versus projected demand. This is the result of the non-value-added activities associated primarily with its execution methods (purchase orders/ work orders, etc.). Manual kanban, on the other hand, is a good execution tool but has absolutely no planning capability. It, too, is riddled with non-value-added activities, primarily in its perpetuation methods (hand recalculations, etc.). The solution is to take the strength of each technique and combine them into a fully automated kanban system that eliminates the non-value-added activities associated with each system. There is a cost associated with the programming of the two calculation modules, MRP enhancements, and kanban containers, but this expense gets a payback from lower inventories, quicker response to customers, and elimination of the cost associated with non-value-added activities of a pure MRP or pure manual kanban system operating by itself.

The AFT system execution and perpetuation methodology is highly automated, yet it is driven and controlled by the user. In addition, a full set of reports and screens keeps the user and suppliers informed of current conditions and exceptions that require user intervention. These reports and screens used to perpetuate the AFT system are the subject of this chapter.

SUPPLIER ONE-LINE-PER-ITEM MRP REPORT

Each time MRP is exploded, a one-line-per-item MRP projection is downloaded to the supplier. The supplier uses this for the sole purpose of resource planning and adjusting the lead-time quantity on their shelf. Figure 8-1 shows the basic format of this report. It lists the OEM's part number and description, the manufacturer's part number (where applicable), and the newly calculated kanban order quantity. The report also shows the current on-order condition along with the projected MRP requirements. The projected MRP requirements are first expressed in weekly and then monthly increments. This MRP projection is a valuable tool in preparing the supplier base to meet the OEM's future demand.

The intent of the report is not to show precise quantities and timing from which ensured orders will be launched, but to give the supplier the best estimate of the OEM's demand levels so they can recalculate the lead-time quantities on their shelf and perform resource planning. Two points need to be made regarding this report:

1. The supplier will sometimes call after reviewing their one-line-per-item MRP download to question an unexpected, large increase in demand or a reduced demand by the OEM. This dialogue should be expected and encouraged.
2. There will be times when the supplier is falling behind in maintaining the lead-time quantities on the shelf. The immediate question from the supplier usually centers around what you expect to be triggering in the next few days by quantity and period. This situation is not acceptable as an everyday occurrence, and the OEM needs to resolve it. It is important to work with the suppliers on these issues, yet there is no

| | | | | | | | November | | | | | | | | |
Part #	Description	Mfg. part number	Kanban order qty.	On order	27	3	10	17	24	Dec. All	Jan. All	Feb. All	Mar. All	April All
105605	Capacitor	C7GEOR71FI8SO	500	0	500	500	500	500	500	1500	2000	2000	2500	2000
316526	Capacitor	HPH9IL639DOES3M	100	100	200	200	200	200	200	600	800	800	1000	900
319879	Capacitor	UC3H85BET8TE3R	3000	3000	6000	6000	6000	5000	4000	12000	16000	16000	20000	16000
343648	IC	L3A4U2RIE523	1000	0	1000	1000	1000	1000	2000	6000	8000	8000	2000	2000
383427	IC	TR78E 9EWO86M	400	400	400	400	400	400	400	1200	0	0	0	0
442743	REGVOLT	AN21BEA83TSU2	8000	8000	8000	8000	8000	8000	8000	24000	32000	32000	34000	34000
483425	RESJ423534	PRA5YNOJA253S	2000	2000	4000	4000	4000	4000	4000	12000	16000	16000	16000	16000
504526	RESJ523859	ON64SHA564NNO	300	300	300	300	400	400	400	1200	1600	1600	2000	1600
553735	CAP	N5A65803KID645	400	400	400	400	400	400	400	1200	1600	1600	2000	1600
679342	CAP	PUM86KI234N23	200	0	200	200	200	200	200	600	800	800	1000	800

MRP Download to Supplier

Supplier XYZ

10/27/97

Figure 8-1. Supplier One Line per Item MRP Report

denying that if your immediate projections are accurate, you will have fewer calls to contend with. This brings up another question: Would a one-line-per-item MRP be more accurate for this purpose if it were based upon gross requirements, net requirements, or planned order releases? We cover each of these options below.

Gross Requirements Report

You can use gross requirements as the projected demand that is downloaded to the suppliers. They can easily determine the average daily demand that provides the base for determining lead-time quantities and resource planning. This information cannot be used to ascertain the precise timing of when kanban will be triggered and due in from the supplier, however, because the gross requirements do not take the OEM's on-hand quantity into consideration. For example, if the one-line-per-item gross requirements MRP download projects the average daily demand to be 100 pieces per day for the first week, there could already be 2,500 pieces in the OEM's facility that may prevent the triggering of kanban for a long time. The one-line-per-item gross requirement MRP is only intended to be used by the supplier for determining lead-time quantities and for resource planning. It is not intended to determine precise quantities and periods when kanban will be triggered and required from the supplier.

Net Requirements Report

The one-line-per-item net requirements MRP report is more accurate than the gross requirements report simply because it subtracts the OEM's on-hand inventory. It still is not a precise representation of the actual periods that kanban will be triggered and due in from the supplier. To demonstrate what would occur under the kanban system versus net MRP, let us use the information from the dual/triple-container kanban simulation example in Figure 7-10, as reflected in Figure 8-2. First, the supplier would have to analyze by hand the one-line-per-item net requirements MRP report, part number by part number, to determine what is believed to be required at the OEM by doing the following (note: the supplier knows that the kanban order quantity is 240 pieces from the downloaded report):

1. The first net requirement of 5 pieces is due at the OEM on day 3. The kanban order quantity is 240 pieces. This requires a delivery to the OEM of 240 pieces (kanban order quantity) on day 3. These 240 pieces will last until a negative of 3 pieces occurs on day 6 (240 pieces minus 5, minus 88, minus 72, minus 78).
2. Delivery of 240 pieces to the OEM on day 6 would last until a negative of 7 pieces occurs on day 9.
3. Delivery of 240 pieces to the OEM on day 9 would last until a negative of 59 pieces occurs on day 13.
4. Delivery of 240 pieces to the OEM on day 13, etc.

The reality of the situation, however, is that the kanban simulation clearly reflects that 240 pieces are due at the OEM on days 3, 5, 8, and 11, not on days 3, 6, 9, and 13 as determined by the one-line-per-item net requirements MRP report. The discrepancy lies in the differences between the MRP and kanban order-launching mechanisms. MRP will launch orders when zero on-hand is projected to occur. Kanban, however, launches orders based upon different criteria, as shown below:

- *Single container.* Order is launched when the total of on-hand and on-order quantities falls below the kanban lot size.
- *Dual container.* Order is launched when a container becomes empty.
- *Multiple container.* Order is launched as soon as consumption begins on the container.

MRP Explosion

- 1 day supplier lead time
- 245 pieces on hand

Day	1	2	3	4	5	6	7	8	9	10	11	12	13	14
Gross requirements	85	90	75	88	72	78	80	85	79	69	70	75	78	85
Net requirements			**5**	**88**	**72**	**78**	**80**	**85**	**79**	**69**	**70**	**75**	**78**	**85**

Dual Kanban Simulation

- 1 day supplier lead time
- 1 day down load frequency
- 240 piece kanban lot size
- 45 pieces kanban 1
- 200 pieces kanban 2

Day	1	2	3	4	5	6	7	8	9	10	11	12	13	14
Kanban 1	0T	0D	**235R**	147	75	0T	0D	**240R**	233	164	94	19	0T	0D
Kanban 2	160	70	0T	0D	**240R**	237	157	72	0T	0D	**240R**	240	181	96

T=Triggered   D=Download   R=Received

Figure 8-2. MRP "Net Requirements" Quantity and Date Compared to Kanban Simulation Receive Quantity and Date

The supplier can use the one-line-per-item net requirement MRP for determining lead-time quantities and for resource planning. It is not intended to determine the precise quantities required by time periods that will be experienced under kanban.

Planned Order Release Report

For suppliers, the one-line-per-item planned order release MRP report is user-friendly (see Figure 8-3). This is because the report lot-sizes MRP's net demands by what will be the kanban order quantity and offsets this based upon supplier lead-time (see "Order Policy Code Field," Chapter 6). It also takes into consideration the OEM's on-hand inventory. The results, however, are identical to those obtained with the net requirements report, except that the supplier will not have to perform the calculations by hand to arrive at the same answer. The supplier can only use the one-line-item per item planned order release MRP for determining lead-time quantities and for resource planning. It cannot be used for determining precise quantities required by time periods that will be experienced under kanban.

All three reports are equally useful for their intended purpose. The key is to understand what you are giving the supplier as it pertains to kanban, and to explain it and its role to the supplier. The broad purpose of the one-line-per-item MRP is to give the supplier the best possible information regarding the OEM's anticipated demand levels to determine lead-time quantities and resource planning. This can be provided for all kanban part numbers.

SUPPLIER KANBAN TRIGGER REPORT

What is obvious from the above discussion is that the kanban simulation is an ideal tool for determining the precise quantities required by time periods that should be experienced under kanban. As shown in Figure 8-4, you can format this report by the date and quantity of what should

MRP Explosion

- 1 day supplier lead time
- 245 pieces on hand

Day	1	2	3	4	5	6	7	8	9	10	11	12	13	14
Gross requirements	85	90	75	88	72	78	80	85	79	69	70	75	78	85
Net requirements			5	88	72	78	80	85	79	69	70	75	78	85
Plan order release		**240**			**240**			**240**			**240**			

Dual Kanban Simulation

- 1 day supplier lead time
- 1 day down load frequency
- 240 piece kanban lot size
- 45 pieces kanban 1
- 200 pieces kanban 2

Day	1	2	3	4	5	6	7	8	9	10	11	12	13	14
Kanban 1	0T	D	0T	0D	**240R**	0T	0D	**240R**	0T	0D	94	19	0T	0D
Kanban 2	160	70	**235R**	147	75	237	157	72	233	164	240	240	181	96

T=Triggered   D=Download   R=Received

Figure 8-3. MRP Plan Order Release Quantity and Timing Compared to Kanban Simulation Receive Quantity and Date

Supplier Kanban Trigger

Supplier XET

10/27/97

Part #	Description	Mfg. part number	Date																		
			1	2	3	4	5	6	7	8	9	10	11	12	13	14	15	16	17	18	19	20
5679	Voltage reg.	VR452765S	240		240			240			240				240			240			240		

Figure 8–4. Supplier Kanban Trigger Report Based on Kanban Simulation

be triggered, or you can base it on the date and quantity due at the OEM. (Again, we use the data from the dual/triple-kanban simulation in Figure 7-10 to demonstrate this report.) From this report, the supplier can easily ascertain exactly what should occur under kanban. The simulation can be highly accurate so long as the demand it was predicated upon occurs. Keep the following in mind:

1. *The kanban simulation does not extend very far into the future.* From a resource-planning standpoint, the supplier will still use the one-line-per-item MRP. For fine tuning the lead-time quantity, however, or for answering specific questions from the supplier on what to expect to be triggered in the next few days by quantity and time period, the supplier trigger report is an excellent tool.

2. *Not all part numbers on kanban are simulated.* What is typically simulated are the kanban items whose replenishment lead times are expressed in full days. In addition, the multiple-container option is usually not simulated; that is, not all kanban part numbers are simulated and available for this report.

MANUFACTURING QUEUE SCREEN

The manufacturing queue screen contains all the manufacturing kanban items that have been triggered but have yet to print a manufacturing traveler (see Figure 8-5). It shows the current work load of the cell that can be stratified by trigger date or due date. On the manufacturing queue screen you will see the triggered part number, its description, quantity due, flag (potential stock-outs indicated by asterisks), trigger date, due date, time due, part status, and hours loaded. The part status is especially important when you deal with assembly work cells because they are based upon a parts-availability simulation. And this parts-availability

Manufacturing Queue   10/27/97

Mechanical assembly—Department 10

Due 10/27

Part number	Description	Qty. due	Flag	Trigger date	Due date	Time due	Part status	Hours loaded
5725649	Bevel assembly	80		10/24/97	10/27/97	0800	OK	17.0 hours
4275349	Rim assembly	50		10/24/97	10/27/97	0826	OK	12.0 hours
3473274	Jack assembly	8		10/24/97	10/27/97	0900	OK	4.0 hours
7325643	Spindle assembly	100		10/24/97	10/27/97	1800	Short CM 56	18.0 hours
								51.0 hours

Due 10/28

Part number	Description	Qty. due	Flag	Trigger date	Due date	Time due	Part status	Hours loaded
6439645	Bar assembly	60		10/27/97	10/28/97	0800	OK	20.5 hours
5474247	Magnet assembly	200		10/27/97	10/28/97	0900	OK	15.0 hours
5725649	Bevel assembly	80		10/27/97	10/28/97	1400	Short 100%	17.0 hours
4245321	Pump assembly	50		10/24/97	10/27/97	1300	OK	22.5 hours
								75.0 hours

Total hours in queue = 126.0

Note: Asterisks would appear under "Flag" if all the containers for a given part number had been triggered.

Figure 8-5. Manufacturing Queue Screen Reflects Priority and Load Hours

simulation informs you whether all the parts are available (OK); whether there is a parts shortage, and the degree to which they are short (100 percent short = nothing can be made); or whether a partial number of units can be made (for example, CM 56 = Can Make 56 units).

By simulating shortages you avoid starting a job and finding out halfway through that there are part shortages. The parts availability simulation runs each night after all the transactions for the current day are entered into the computer. The screen displays the total operator hours needed for each cell. When the operators are ready to build the item, they will generate a bar-coded manufacturing traveler. When the bar-coded manufacturing traveler is printed, the specific item comes off the screen and the total operator hours needed for each cell is updated. This work load information is essential for the supervisor or self-directed work teams in shifting operators to the appropriate cells. You can employ three other options in the manufacturing queue screen:

1. You can have the MRP dispatch report for non-kanban items appear on the same screen if the part is produced in that specific cell. The common denominator between non-kanban items and kanban items is their due dates. You may need this feature, since often there are part numbers that are not candidates for kanban. Also, by using this option you eliminate the need for the work cell to use more than one report or screen.

2. In this option the triggered kanban part numbers on the screen are prioritized and stratified according to the one that needs replenishment first (not by due date). For example, if one kanban item has a kanban lot size of 100 pieces and has 70 pieces available, it would have a 70% availability. If another kanban item has a kanban lot size of 300 pieces and has 150 pieces available, it would have a 50% availability. The screen would list the kanban item with a 50% availability first and the kanban item with 70% next. This method has

been practiced for years under the order point methodology. It applies the resources where they are most needed.

3. Under the part status portion of the screen, the manufacturing queue screen can list the supporting part numbers of the parent that are simulated to be short. It can even accommodate supplier or manufacturing commitment dates that are inputted into the system by the buyer or work cell responsible for providing the replenishment.

Some companies generate a hard copy report similar to these screens to help them assess the work load for each cell at the beginning of each morning. In the end, the architecture of system capabilities that a company chooses will depend upon the specific environment that the automated kanban methodology is placed in.

PURCHASING AND MANUFACTURING SHORTAGE REPORTS

When the parts availability simulation is performed for the manufacturing queue screen, it picks up the anticipated shortages and places them on a shortage report. There is one shortage report for purchasing and one for manufacturing. These reports are usually printed each morning.

Purchasing shortage report. The AFT system places buy items simulated to be short on a purchasing shortage report. The report is organized according to the responsible suppliers (see Figure 8-6). It lists the part number that is expected to be short, as well as the description, quantity short, date required, quantity open on the purchase order, purchase order number, due date, and last commitment date given by the supplier. You can then input this information into the MRPII system, where it will then appear on the manufacturing queue screen under the part status.

Purchasing Shortage   10/27/97

Supplier B   Phone (714) 488-2469   **Contact: Jason Joseph**

Part number	Description	Quantity short	Date required	Qty.	P.O. number	Open purchase orders Due	Last commitment
153865	Spindle	44	10/24/97	100	56342-20	10/23/97	10/24/97

Supplier C   Phone (714) 488-2472   **Contact: Shannon Christine**

Part number	Description	Quantity short	Date required	Qty.	P.O. number	Open purchase orders Due	Last commitment
167435	Gear mount	300	10/23/97	400	56345-20	10/22/97	10/27/97

Manufacturing Shortage   10/27/97

Required from department 15

Part number	Description	Quantity short	Date required	Qty.	W.O. number	Due	Days late
158769	Bevel	80	10/27/97	100	56342-20	10/26/97	1

Figure 8-6. Purchasing and Manufacturing Shortage Report

Manufacturing shortage report. The make items that AFT simulates to be short are listed on the manufacturing shortage report according to the department responsible for making the replenishment. The report lists the part number simulated to be short, description, quantity short, date required, and current open work order information, if one exists. The individual departments can use an optional feature whereby they can input into MRP their commitment dates for each item appearing in the report. They can control this report regarding the distance in time, for example, one or two days. The confirmed dates will then appear on the manufacturing queue screen, where the item is simulated to be short.

The parts availability simulation is a vital tool because there is no kitting (stockroom pull) to determine shortages prior to a run. Without simulation, capability shortage racks of incomplete build items will begin to appear throughout the facility.

FLEXIBLE WORK-CELL STAFFING REPORT

In a flexible work cell, the number of operators is adjusted up or down to compensate for fluctuation in the average daily demand. AFT determines staffing levels by automatically calculating the required number of operators for each cell each time that MRP is exploded. The AFT system generates by work cell the flexible work-cell staffing report (see Figure 8-7). It reflects the flexible work cell's part numbers (that have an average daily demand), description, the average daily demand, labor content per unit, and the extended total of average daily demand times the labor content per unit. The extended total is then added and divided by the operators' effective time per day to determine the number of operators required in the cell each day. AFT reflects the grand total number of operators that will be required to support all the flexible work cells.

The flexible work-cell staffing report is accurate providing that there is an *average daily build*. The more the demand is lot-sized with excessive lead times and safety stock, the less meaningful this report becomes.

	Flexible Work Cell Staffing			10/27/97
	Department 5—Base machine cell			
Part number	Description	ADD	Labor content per unit	Extended total
4327562	Base bevel	600	.80	480.0 minutes
4683245	Base flat	400	.75	300.0 minutes
4894356	Base square	600	.95	570.0 minutes
				1350.0 minutes per day/460 effective time = **2.93 people**
	Department 6—Lever machine cell			
Part number	Description	ADD	Labor content per unit	Extended total
4327562	Base Bevel	900	2.00	1800.0 minutes
				1800.0 minutes per day/460 effective time = **3.91 people**
			Grand total = 6.84 people per day required	

Figure 8-7. Flexible Work-Cell Staffing Report

Also, the report is not very meaningful unless the majority of the items in the work cell are kanban items. The more you stray away from the purity of kanban (not implementing the prerequisites), the more difficult it is to operate it. If you have yet to implement the kanban prerequisites, or if you have a strong mix of kanban and non-kanban items (90% of the total daily hours within the flexible cell should have a daily build), the MRPII capacity load report may be the best tool to use for projecting staffing levels. Your kanban items will still appear on the capacity load report, since their requirements are exploded all the way through to the lowest level component during the MRP explosion.

ADD/SUBTRACT MULTIPLE CONTAINER REPORT

The logic for this report was covered in Chapter 6. The AFT system automatically makes adjustments to the number of containers required for each nonflexible work-cell kanban item and purchase kanban item. This occurs each time MRP is exploded. AFT system adjustments are then reflected on the add/subtract multiple-container report, which is sorted by department number. One purpose of this report is to alert the department head about the degree to which demand is shifting (see Figure 8-8).

ADJUST KANBAN REPORT FOR SINGLE CONTAINER

This report is designed for the single-container option. It results from the kanban simulation being alerted that a front load (a stock-out within replenishment lead time) has occurred. It advises the responsible buyer to contact the supplier to determine how the situation can best be handled (see Figure 8-9).

TRIGGER KANBAN REPORT FOR DUAL/TRIPLE-CONTAINER OPTION

The AFT system is alerted through the kanban simulation that a front load has occurred and that both containers are currently in-house. The action required is for the using department to empty one container into the other and trigger a replenishment immediately. This report is sorted in several ways:

- The department that houses the components will receive a copy of this report, sorted by department number, and they will trigger the container.
- Each individual buyer will receive this report, which is first sorted by buyer, then supplier, to enable the buyer to contact the supplier to determine how this situation can best be handled.
- Each production planner will receive a copy of this report, sorted by department number, to be able to stay on top of the situation.

Add/Subtract Multiple Container 10/27/97

Machine department 3

Part number	Description	Current number of containers	+ Qty. left in adjust file	=	Qty. of containers in circulation	Vs.	Current number of containers	Add/Sub	Trigger	Qty. in queue/ Hold file	Subtract from queue/ Hold file	New qty. determined/ adjust file
56432	Bearing	24	2		26		25	−1	–	0	0	1
54845	Flange	60	0		60		46	−14	–	15	14	0
54761	Ring	45	4		49		55	+6	6	0	0	0
65434	Shaft	35	0		35		40	+5	5	20	0	0
74327	Rotor	25	5		30		28	−2	0	0	0	2
87564	Flange	60	10		70		75	+5	5	0	0	0
					270		269					

Figure 8-8. Add/Subtract Multiple Container Report

Buyer Joan				**Adjust Kanban—Single Container**				10/27/97
	Supplier R	**Contact: Jim Sanders**			**Phone number (714) 488-2483**			
Part number	Description	MRP day	MRP gross	New kanban lot size	Quantity on hand	PO number	P.O. qty.	P.O. due date
563098	Saddle	10/27	3000	7500	3010	Action required		
		10/28	7500					
		10/29	2300					
		10/30	2500					
267385	Clamp	10/27	250	950	400	53565-23	400	10/28/97
		10/28	950			Action required		
		10/29	260					
		10/30	235					

Figure 8-9. Adjust Kanban—Single Container Report

Buyer Jim				**Trigger Kanban—Dual/Triple**			10/27/97
	Supplier Y		**Contact: Phil George**		**Phone number (503) 621-8132**		
Floor location	Part number	Description	MRP day	MRP gross	New kanban lot size	Quantity on hand	
Mech134	176834	Spacer	10/27	800	800	390	
			10/28	120			
			10/29	125			
			10/30	122			
Mech232	185643	Lever	10/27	100	700	550	
			10/28	115			
			10/29	700			
			10/30	120			

Figure 8-10. Trigger Kanban—Dual/Triple Report

Figure 8-10 shows a basic trigger kanban report for a dual/triple-container option report. This example sorts by department and shows the floor location of all the containers requiring action. It lists the part number, description, the MRP day, and the MRP gross quantities. The front load of 800 is on day 10/27. The new kanban lot size of 800 matches the front load, and what needs to occur is made evident with only 390 pieces on hand.

Buyer Phil				Adjust Kanban—Dual/Triple				10/27/97
Supplier X			Contact: Laurie Roley		Phone number (202) 932-8142			
Part number	Description	MRP day	MRP gross	New kanban lot size	Quantity on hand	PO number	P.O. qty.	P.O. due date
237453	Piston	10/27	2000	8000	3000	55463–42	4000	10/29/97
		10/28	8000					
		10/29	2100					
		10/30	2400					
267385	Rod	10/27	150	850	350	55567–22	400	10/28/97
		10/28	850					
		10/29	140					
		10/30	135					

Figure 8-11. Adjust Kanban—Dual/Triple Report

ADJUST KANBAN REPORT FOR DUAL/TRIPLE-CONTAINER OPTION

It is through the kanban simulation that the AFT system is also alerted when a front load occurs and that one container has already been triggered. The action required is for the responsible buyer to contact the supplier and have them increase the order size and to bring it in earlier if required (see Figure 8-11). This report is sorted by buyer then supplier, thus enabling the buyer to contact the supplier for immediate action. It is also sorted by the production planner to help everyone stay on top of the situation.

PURCHASING KANBAN DUE REPORT

This report breaks down by supplier all the kanban orders that have been triggered and are currently open (see Figure 8-12). It lists the part number, description, open purchase order number, kanban order quantity, downloaded date, due date, days late, and if there is a potential stock-out due to all the containers being triggered. If there is a potential stock-out,

Supplier B				Purchasing Kanban Due				10/27/97
Part number	Description	P.O. number	Kanban order quantity	Download date	Due date	Days late	Stock out	Flag
153865	Spindle	56342-20	100	10/21/97	10/23/97	2	Yes	*
153865	Spindle	56342-21	800	10/23/97	10/27/97	0	Yes	*
5784532	Spacer	56863-15	1500	10/24/97	10/28/97	0	No	
6353687	Lever	56856-30	130	10/24/97	10/28/97	0	No	

Overall performance rating = 92% (.95 × .98 × .99 × 100)

On-time delivery		Received full quantity		Quality	
Kanbans received to date	200	Kanbans received to date	200	Kanbans received to date	200
Kanbans received on time	190	Kanbans received full	196	Kanbans accepted	198
On-time delivery %	95%	Received full %	98%	Quality %	99%

Figure 8-12. Purchasing Kanban Due Report

an asterisk will appear under the heading of "Flag." This, of course, warrants special attention. This report also provides an overall supplier rating that is extremely useful in encouraging better supplier performance or in complimenting their performance. It is important that this supplier rating be available to the buyers at all times so that whenever contact is made with the supplier, performance levels can be continuously evaluated and discussed. Requiring and achieving high supplier performance is not project-oriented or a one-time effort. The OEM must be consistent in expecting and working with the supplier to attain a high level of performance. The overall performance rating is derived by multiplying the *on-time delivery performance* (calculated as a decimal) by the *received full quantity* by the *quality*. These performance figures are an accumulation of the supplier's receipts to date.

It is also vital that the report be credible and up-to-date. For example, when receipts come in the back door you should receive and input them into the computer the same day. Without a credible report there is no improvement, only reaction.

SUPPLIER PERFORMANCE RATING REPORT

This report measures the supplier's performance by the month (see Figure 8-13). The purpose of the report is to track any trends (good or bad) that may be developing with a supplier. If the supplier performance rating begins to fall, you need to investigate immediately—maybe there is new management, or an overload situation, or maybe the company is getting into financial problems. If the trend shows that the supplier performance is improving, let them know.

Everything covered in this chapter will not be applied in the same way from company to company. Since each manufacturing facility will develop an automated kanban version to meet the needs of their specific environment, the design of these reports and screens will vary.

Buyer Chuck Elias		**Supplier Performance Rating**				10/27/97
		Overall supplier rating				
Supplier	October	September	August	July	June	May
S	68%	67%	62%	50%	62%	61%
I	82%	85%	90%	95%	96%	98%
K	85%	80%	75%	70%	69%	70%
U	87%	86%	88%	85%	87%	84%
O	94%	97%	96%	93%	96%	93%
C	97%	97%	96%	98%	97%	99%
P	98%	99%	97%	98%	98%	97%
L	99%	98%	100%	99%	100%	99%

Figure 8-13. Supplier Performance Rating Report

What is important is that everyone understands the basic concepts underlying the automated kanban system so they can intelligently select, create, design, test, and gradually implement their own automated version. The next chapter shows how kanban can be applied to different types of environments.

9

key topics of the automated
kanban system

aving your automated kanban system control literally thousands of part numbers effectively is an extremely rewarding experience. This is the result of a thorough design process that begins with visualizing how the automated kanban system will operate within its intended environment. You need to consider key operational functions and tasks in the design phase, such as managing the transportation costs, mistake-proofing the triggering of kanban, and handling non-work-cell kanban items. You will handle some of these operational topics through procedures and others by system design. In this chapter we cover these key operational topics and then provide a general guideline of the automated kanban system design process.

MANAGING THE TRANSPORTATION COST

Requesting frequent supplier deliveries should result in lower inventories. There is a down side, however: Your transportation and handling costs will increase if this is done without forethought or technique. This is why you must thoroughly study the pros and cons of the frequency of supplier deliveries prior to implementing kanban. What you want to take into consideration is the increase in delivery costs and handling costs versus the decrease in carrying cost achieved by lowering your inventory. The following are a few techniques that you can employ to lower the overall inventory while minimizing transportation and handling costs.

1. *Perform an A, B, C analysis.* The highly expensive items are the A items, which usually represent 20% of the part numbers and equate to 80% of the overall inventory dollars. The inexpensive items are the C items, which typically represent 50% of the part numbers and equate to 5% of the overall dollars. Where it makes sense, you should set the A items for frequent deliveries and the C items for infrequent deliveries.

2. *Create bulk shipments.* The supplier lead time for a given supplier is the same regardless of the individual component. The supplier lead time is the amount of time the supplier requires to box and transport the items to the OEM once they receive the download. For inexpensive components, the download frequency in the AFT system can be set for longer periods of time (for example, once every four weeks). What will occur is a buildup of triggered demand for the specific supplier. When the download occurs, all the required items will have the same due date, thus enabling a bulk shipment. This not only reduces the cost of transportation but enables the user to control handling cost.

MISTAKE-PROOF THE AFT TRIGGERING CAPABILITY

At all times the AFT system keeps track of the number of containers in play and how many containers are currently triggered. To prevent the user from triggering more containers than what is assigned, you should mistake-proof the AFT system. This is done by programming the system to prevent a user from triggering more containers than what is assigned to the specific part number.

NON-WORK-CELL KANBAN ITEMS

Typically, all the machinery required to produce a given item is housed in the work cell responsible for replenishment. The build begins at the start of the work cell and is completed at the end of the cell. The work cell's completed item is then delivered and stored at its point of use. When the item is triggered again, it appears on the manufacturing queue screen at the work cell responsible for replenishment, and the process begins anew. This is straightforward. The process becomes a little unclear when all the machinery necessary to produce a given item is not located in a specific cell. Some practitioners try to overcome this by taking kanban items that are in different stages of completion and storing them at these external machine sites (see Figure 9-1). Some practitioners even assign dash numbers to the base number in an attempt to control this

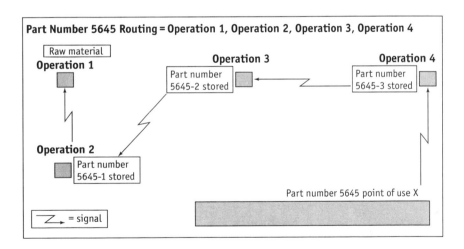

Figure 9-1. Permanent Multiple Storage Sites for the Same Part Number at Different Levels of Completion.

This becomes complex for non-work cell kanban applications. In the above scenario the point of use triggers a requirement at operation 4. Operation 4 stores operation 3 items at its site. When consumption takes place on operation 3 items (stored at operation 4) a replenishment order is generated at operation 3 to produce more. This cascades all the way down to the raw material at operation 1.

method of producing a build. This scenario has turned what is supposed to be a simple system into a very complex one. Now that your control points are spread out, you must maintain the integrity of new part numbers, and cycle-counting on the floor is more involved.

Other options are to (1) maintain the completed item at the point of use, (2) trigger the requirement at operation 1, and (3) print out a barcoded traveler at operation 1 that reflects the routing. If it is an assembly item, you can code each operation as a deduct point. This will immediately subtract the inventory of the supporting components that are consumed. This method simplifies the situation.

REACTING TO CUSTOMER DEMAND VERSUS PRODUCING TO A FROZEN SCHEDULE

Without hesitation, the goal of a world-class manufacturer is to be able to respond to customer demand quickly and effectively. You cannot do this if you impose a frozen master schedule on your replenishment system. A frozen master schedule simply reflects the inability of the organization to respond to shifting demand and in turn adversely impacts the customer. This is why properly implementing the kanban prerequisites is the first step in an organization's becoming highly responsive to the customer. Once you put these prerequisites into place, your lead times will dramatically drop from weeks to days or even hours. Although the manufacturer often has no choice but to start off with a frozen master schedule, they must remember that this should be a temporary solution until world-class capabilities are achieved.

STANDARD PRODUCT FINISHED GOODS/ALLOCATION METHODOLOGY

As a rule, you should maintain a finished-goods inventory on the shelf if your customers expect immediate delivery when placing an order and if your internal operation is unable to respond sufficiently and quickly.

In this case you would handle the finished-goods inventory as a kanban item, and the AFT system would automatically calculate the kanban lot size. You usually employ a single-container discrete option for finished-goods items. In addition, when the kanban order is booked, the AFT system employs an allocation methodology that immediately subtracts the finished-goods inventory. In other words, consumption occurs through the booking of the order. This facilitates the initiation of the replenishment order instead of waiting for it to ship.

NONLINEAR CUSTOMER DEMAND

As a rule, the broader the customer base, the more linear the demand patterns. When a company is dealing with only a handful of customers, the demand patterns can potentially be nonlinear. It is important to make a distinction between genuine nonlinear demand and artificially created nonlinear demand. Genuine nonlinear demand is usually project-related, such as door locks are to a building contractor who is engaged in a specific housing development. Artificially created nonlinear demand is usually the result of the OEM for years building in batches with long lead times and the customers buying in this same batch-building pattern. This is why the OEM should show the new manufacturing capabilities to their customers as soon as they have improved their internal capabilities by employing the kanban prerequisites. The OEM's customers need to know that they can now respond to smaller, as-needed customer requirements. Everyone wants to lower their inventory levels. Most would prefer consistent, steady, and smaller order sizes rather than single large hits. The customer benefits because they can now carry less inventory, and the OEM benefits by having a more linear operation. Most practitioners know that sporadic large orders force overtime and the engagement of temporary workers, which impacts negatively on quality and increases costs. It is worth your time to investigate and analyze your customer demand patterns. You cannot assume they are unalterable—find out.

IMBALANCE OF INVENTORY

Implementing kanban is a gradual process. It begins with the OEM at the final assembly level and works its way down to purchased components. What usually occurs is an imbalance of inventory until the majority of the items are on kanban. An imbalance of inventory means that there is a very noticeable difference in the part set count. For example, if part numbers B and C are used in final product A, there may be a lot more of part number B on-hand (because it is on MRP) than of part number C (which may be on kanban). This is a normal phase of kanban implementation.

What usually creates this situation for part number B is an overly optimistic sales forecast inflating the MRP projection coupled with long lead times. Kanban items, on the other hand, have a much shorter lead time and only react to consumption. Although an inflated master schedule can inflate the kanban lot size, the inventory is still much closer to what it should be than if it was being procured through MRP. The good news in this scenario is that at least the C part number is on kanban rather than MRP. Otherwise, the inventory could be inflated on both part numbers. Although this situation is not part of the design process, it is an effect that the design team should be aware of and expect as they monitor the inventory during kanban implementation.

HIGH DEGREE OF COMMONALITY

In a number of situations, the demand patterns and/or uniqueness of the final product make it unfavorable for kanban. However, if there is a high degree of commonality among components at the lower levels, the demand patterns for these lower-level components will tend to smooth out—making them potential candidates for kanban. A good example of this is in the electronics industry, whose lower-level components are things such as resistors and capacitors. Although the board assemblies that they go into could be nonlinear, the components themselves could end up being linear due to their commonality.

BROADCAST APPLICATION

You usually apply the broadcast application within the OEM's facility, but you can effectively use it with the supplier base in certain applications. For example, if the OEM is going to lose sales because they cannot immediately ship the product after it is booked, they probably would want to carry finished-goods inventory on the shelf. If the finished-goods item's replenishment lead-time to manufacture is two days, it will force the OEM to carry two days' worth of finished goods plus safety stock for variation in demand. Under this scenario, inventory to the OEM is more valuable at the finished-goods level than the component level, because the finished goods are immediately available to the customer. An OEM may choose to carry extra finished goods beyond the replenishment lead time and safety stock as long as they do not have to carry expensive components on-hand as well. If the supplier of the expensive components is close by and can deliver within a short time (for example, one day) after a download, the component's total replenishment lead time may be factored into the OEM's level of finished goods they are carrying on the shelf (now three days total plus safety stock). When the total of on-hand and on-order of the finished-goods item falls below the calculated kanban lot size (single order discrete), the AFT system will automatically generate and download a purchase order to the supplier for the expensive component. Since there are enough finished goods on hand, you have enough time (one day) for the expensive components to arrive so you can manufacture (two days) the finished-goods item and place it on the shelf. (See the "Precision Tape Backup" example in Chapter 10.)

SHORT RECEIPT POLICY

With the dual/triple-container option, there should only be one supplier receipt permitted per order. If 1,000 pieces are triggered and downloaded to the supplier and they deliver a partial shipment of 600 pieces, the AFT system will generate a receipt for 600 pieces and automatically cancel the balance of the order. In this example, 600 pieces residing in a container versus the needed 1,000 pieces will more than likely create a stock-out. To avoid this, empty the partial receipt (in this case, 600 pieces) into the other container and re-trigger. You do this because the supplier does not have a container to ship the balance of 400 pieces. The issue is not whether the OEM should receive the partial shipment, but rather what the supplier is going to do about shipping short. Frequent partial shipments can quickly become a serious problem, so consider this criterion carefully when evaluating your suppliers.

Since the single-container option does not involve a container in the transport and receipt of material, the OEM can accept a partial shipment and keep the balance of the order open, if desired, without concern for what the supplier will use to ship the residual. With the multiple-container option, the receipt is usually closed out short and the container is placed in front of the other containers at the point of use.

Procedures for dealing with short shipments differ for each company. They depend upon a number of factors, including

- Degree of safety stock usually applied
- Historical relationship between projected demand levels and actual demand levels
- Scarcity of the components in question

If it is possible, it is usually best to have one policy for each container type. It is too time consuming to analyze each supplier receipt that is short. Most suppliers are pretty good at hitting the specific quantities and due dates. Just make sure you have reasonable policies in place to deal with short shipments and that your suppliers are aware of these policies.

FREQUENCY OF KANBAN RECALCULATION

The ebb and flow of business differs from one manufacturing environment to another. At one extreme are companies that experience minimal shifts in demand throughout the year. Their demand is fairly linear and predictable. This type of manufacturing environment usually recalculates kanban lot sizes infrequently. At the other extreme are manufacturing environments that lack visibility and predictability; these environments are usually forced to recalculate kanban lot sizes frequently. However, there are other factors that are not as apparent as fluctuations in demand that can impact your kanban lot sizes: for instance, bill of material modifications due to engineering changes. You can wisely avert a potential stock-out with the little effort it takes to recalculate. If, on the other hand, there are no changes, no action is required.

IMPACT OF NOT LOT-SIZING MRP

You may be tempted to minimize your programming by not lot-sizing MRP's planned order releases according to the newly calculated kanban lot sizes. This can potentially create a stock-out. For example, if the MRP demand for a subassembly is 10 pieces per day with a replenishment lead time of four days and no safety stock, its kanban lot size will be 40 pieces. These 40 pieces will reside at the point of use. When it is triggered by an upper level consumption, a lot size of 40 pieces will have to be made if you are using a dual kanban container. Let's assume that the lower level supporting component is also a kanban item stationed at the point of use at the subassembly cell. The demand in MRP will show 10 pieces per day for this supporting component, since the planned order release of the subassembly was not lot-sized. Let's also assume that the supporting component has a replenishment lead time of one day with no safety stock. Its kanban lot size is 10 pieces and there are 10 pieces located at the point of use. When the subassembly cell goes to build the 40 pieces as one lot size, it will only have 10 pieces of the lower level supporting component available. The result is a stock-out.

The four-day lead time of the subassembly could easily consist mostly of queue time (waiting for its turn to run as other items are being built) and in actuality all 40 pieces are built in one day. If the subassembly MRP planned order releases were lot-sized according to the newly calculated kanban lot size of 40 pieces, the lower level supporting components' gross requirement would reflect the 40-piece kanban lot-size demand. The AFT calculation routine and the simulation would capture this 40-piece gross requirement and elevate the supporting component kanban lot size to 40 pieces. This would avert a stock-out.

AUTOMATED KANBAN SYSTEM DESIGN PROCESS—GENERAL GUIDELINE

Although no two automated kanban systems are designed the same, there is a general guideline on how to design a fully automated kanban system.

From start to finish, it takes a team to make an automated kanban system happen. Representatives from sales, MIS, manufacturing, materials, and purchasing need to participate in the automated kanban design from its inception. All must agree and feel comfortable with what is being designed. They need to analyze the feasibility, scope of the work, and preliminary cost/benefit ratio prior to the automated kanban design. Generally, the team should ask the following series of questions:

1. What are the key operating issues now with the current system?
2. How linear are the customer orders? Do we need finished-goods kanban? How much finished-goods inventory will we have compared to now?

3. How linear is the demand for the lower level assemblies and components? What will be the average inventory under an automated kanban versus the current method?

4. What is the estimated percentage of part numbers that are candidates for kanban? Is it 5% or 80%? Do we have enough kanban candidates to justify an automated kanban system?

5. How strong is the supplier base?

6. Can we reduce the number of suppliers? Should they be reduced?

7. How willing are the suppliers to go on a kanban system with us?

The following are suggested approaches to help a team answer these questions.

Identify the root cause of what is wrong with the current system. Is it something that will be repeated regardless of the type of system that is put into place? Examples include not perpetuating inventory accurately; suppliers are always late; bills of material are inaccurate. The team needs to acquire and analyze the necessary data to build a profile of the company's present state.

Looking back at least a year, the team needs to study the day-by-day customer bookings of orders to determine how smooth it is. If it is nonlinear, they need to find out why and determine whether there is anything they can do about it. If nothing can be done, the team should look at the MRP's assemblies, subassemblies, and, finally, components. Are the demand patterns smooth? Does the MRP reflect the actual demand quantities and patterns that do occur on the floor? The data have to be reasonably accurate in order to be used as an analytical tool for this stage of the analysis. If the data are not reliable, the team has to make a master schedule based on the actual booking quantities and due dates of past incoming orders and explode it for analysis.

The team needs to decide whether it is necessary to keep finished goods on the shelf. If you need finished goods, you need to calculate kanban lot sizes by hand and then use the historical bookings per day to perform a simulation. Do you stock out? Do you need more safety stock at the finished-goods level? If so, add the safety stock. If there is no stock-out, determine the dollar value of the average finished-goods inventory in the simulation. Is it higher or lower than what you are currently carrying? For this analysis to be meaningful, you need a large enough sample of finished-goods part numbers.

The team needs to calculate kanban lot sizes by hand for assemblies, subassemblies, and components, then perform simulation. Add safety stock if required. Determine the dollar value of the average inventory. Is it higher or lower than what is currently being carried? For this analysis to be meaningful, you need a large enough sample of component part numbers.

The team should determine the accuracy of the bills of material, inventory, and the perpetuation of on-order situations. Study the performance of the supplier base to determine on-time delivery record, full receipts versus partial receipts, and quality. How many suppliers do you use? Can you curtail the quantity you use?

The team needs to find out whether yearly purchasing contracts are currently in place. If there aren't any in place, you can achieve cost savings by going to yearly contracts.

The team should also estimate the cost of containers, the cost of hardware (terminals/printers), and differences in transportation costs. It is important that they also estimate the benefits of reduced inventory and the elimination of non-value-added activities. Once the team has accomplished the above, the company should have a reasonable grasp on the scope of the work necessary and the cost/benefits of converting to an automated kanban system. From this point on the team needs to ask specific questions to help formulate a sketch of the overall design of the automated kanban system. These questions should include

1. What will each report look like?
2. Will you simulate the kanban lot size?

3. How will the kanban be triggered?

4. How will the signal reach the work cell responsible for replenishment? Will the current load in hours be available for each work cell?

5. How will the work cell know where to take the items they just built?

6. How will the system handle a mix of kanban and non-kanban items from both a purchasing-procurement and floor-scheduling standpoint?

7. Will triggered purchase requirements be downloaded? If so, how?

8. Will a projection of requirements be sent to the supplier for resource planning and adjustments in lead-time quantity?

9. How will the receipts be performed at the receiving door?

10. Will you count the incoming material? If so, how?

11. How will the receiving department know where to take the material after receipt?

12. What are the exception reports required for the manufacturing and purchasing departments?

Once the team lays out a basic sketch, it can fill in the details regarding logic and reports. A good aid in monitoring implementation is to use an implementation milestone chart reflecting tasks, responsibilities, and timing.

It does take time and effort to design, implement, and perpetuate an automated kanban system properly. There are no safe shortcuts, but the payback for the effort of doing each task correctly is usually immense. The penalty for short-changing the process can be unpleasant. The important point to remember is that in automated kanban, each system will be different for each company. AFT must be tailored to meet the needs of the specific environment in which it is intended to operate. In the next chapter we explore the experiences of three different types of companies that implemented AFT.

10

three examples of AFT implementation

ach company is unique in its competitive position, products offered, manufacturing process capabilities, internal skill base, supplier locations, and management policy. Because of these differences in company environments, the way each kanban system is designed to function will also be unique, though the basics remain the same for building its foundation. The key to developing your own kanban system is to understand these basics, plan the system, design as a team, manually test the methodologies on a few part numbers, automate, test again, gradually implement, and monitor closely. These steps have been put to use at a number of facilities and have yielded significant results. In this chapter, we demonstrate the diversity of design and application of the automated kanban system by looking at the experiences of three companies.

NORTH STAR

An important electrical telecommunications manufacturer in North America, let's call them North Star, was beginning to fall behind the competition in their ability to deliver goods. They had shortage meetings every day that would last one to two hours. They relied heavily upon overtime hours, temporary employees, and out-sourcing to overcome the fluctuation of demand that was compounded by its existing non-value-added activities. Their major concern was how many hot purchase orders had to be realigned and launched and how many kits needed to be pulled each time MRP exploded. If the number of manufacturing hours exceeded internal capacity, they had to out-source the work. These excessive work loads, primarily in the board assembly area (labor-intensive both in direct and indirect hours), involved more kit pulls, which meant the stockroom had to determine the number of temporary workers to use as well as deal with the overtime issues in handling the extra load.

Product profile. North Star offers numerous product options at the finished-goods level. There is a high degree of commonality among assemblies, subassemblies, and components. These consist of harnesses, cables, board assemblies, and mechanical assemblies. Their bills of material prior to JIT implementation was seven levels deep. Their lead time for the final product was four to six weeks. This company has a superior product but their cost and delivery time was higher than the competition.

Component profile. North Star had a total of 9,000 active part numbers, of which approximately 70% were buy components. They procured electronic, machined, and fabricated components that had an average supplier lead time of six weeks. Their electronic distributors were located throughout the United States and the machine and fabrication shops were within a 150-mile radius. Their facility also housed an internal machine shop. Prior to implementing the automated kanban system, they used the MRPII package to buy their components. Their inventory turn ratio was around four turns.

North Star manufacturing methodology. North Star had a traditional plant layout with a stockroom employing 15 full-time clerks. During rush periods, they added as many as 11 temporary clerks to compensate for the extra load. Everything was funneled through the stockroom. Inventory became extremely inaccurate when they brought in temporary clerks. Much of this was due to the lack of training. The major bottle-neck always occurred with the board assembly line. Their lead time was four to six weeks, and they were responsible for making more than 300 different board assembly parts. Like everyone else in the company, they had to build in batches to minimize the frequency of kit pulls and setups.

Action taken to implement automated kanban. The board assembly department was fragmented and the manufacturing methodology needed serious attention, so the board assembly department constructed a work cell that accommodated as many as 20 people with components (1,700 part numbers) located at the point of use in front of the operator. The board assembly department then placed the replenishment components in kanban containers and placed them directly behind the operator. They flattened the number of levels in the bills of material and implemented deduct points and backflushing capability.

They also eliminated all setup time. For example, they used five semiautomatic insertion machines wherein each machine housed 99 part numbers that were in trays located in the machine. The operator pressed a foot pedal after inserting the proper quantity of a part number on the board assembly. This would activate the machine to bring up the next appropriate part number. The machine was programmed to bring the parts up in a sequence specific to the board assembly that was being built. Each machine would work on a different board assembly. Once the batch run of that board assembly was completed, the trays were taken out of the machine and reloaded with the next series of trays for the next board assembly that was to be built.

Setup was eliminated on these machines by placing the machines in a series—one machine after the other, tightly fitted and connected with a rail on which the individual board assemblies being built could slide from machine to machine. The part numbers in the trays were perma-nently assigned for high-volume components. Now each of the five semiautomatic machines builds a portion of any board assembly. The operator does not have to remove the tray. Replenishment kanban containers were also set up directly behind the operator of the semiautomatic machine. The operator can now refill the machine trays by running through the sequence of the 99 components and replenishing them. With these and other enhancements, this production line can run any board assembly in less than four hours, one part number after another, in one-piece lots. All the components that once were in the stockroom now are carried on the board assembly line, and all part numbers coming in from the outside that belong to the board assembly line are routed directly to the point of use via the bar-coded purchasing receipt traveler.

North Star also constructed work cells throughout the facility. Now all the cells responsible for final product have the required assemblies located at the point of use. When consumption occurs, it triggers a manufacturing bar-coded traveler at the start of the line that is responsible for replenishment. The final product is now made within the same day.

In parallel to developing and constructing work cells, North Star was having the AFT system designed for their specific application. After testing it manually for three months, a KCSP was programmed to run on a $3\frac{1}{2}$ inch floppy disk for a PC. The disk contained 500 part numbers with their gross requirements (after MRP was exploded) and other attributes that were downloaded from the mainframe. The KCSP was programmed to test the AFT system that was tailored for their specific application and to drive a sample kanban implementation. They used the PC-based program for three months to test the system design. It was also augmented by another $3\frac{1}{2}$ inch floppy disk program that tracked the movement of the containers to and from the suppliers. Once the specific model designed for their facility proved itself superior to MRP, it was programmed on the mainframe to integrate with the MRPII. The AFT system on the mainframe was tested, monitored, and debugged. Once North Star was satisfied with the testing results, they began their kanban implementation.

Kanban implementation begins. Now when North Star's MRP explodes, their kanban lot sizes are automatically recalculated and consumption triggers replenishment. Also their replenishment orders and one-line-per-item MRP are downloaded to the supplier base. They have improved their relations with their suppliers by working with them on programs such as quick-setup and by negotiating yearly contracts. Because the suppliers were placed on contracts and kanban one at a time, they are no longer pitted against each other from a bidding standpoint. The suppliers retain business as long as their performance remains high and they do not increase pricing. North Star now has over 6,000 part numbers on kanban with suppliers located throughout the United States. Their lead time with the suppliers went from a six-week average to a four-day average. Furthermore, the purchase receipts are placed on a modified electronic scale while the components reside in their respective kanban container. Now when they scan the affixed bar code on the container, it automatically determines the quantity in the container. If the quantity in the container is in tolerance with what was ordered (both quantities are displayed on the computer terminal), the receiving clerk scans the "yes" bar code located near the terminal. This in turn automatically engages the AFT system to transact the receipt.

They also permanently affixed an enlarged picture of the component to the container so the floor operators can check the parts prior to putting the material away. This has dramatically reduced the need for having the electronic components routed to the inspection department. Now many of the machine and fabricated components are delivered directly to the point of use without inspection. Components that are not authorized to go directly to the floor are coded as requiring inspection. Upon receipt, the bar-coded purchasing receipt traveler indicates that the incoming material should be delivered to the inspection department.

Finally, triggered make items now appear on the manufacturing queue screen. When the operator is ready to run the item, a bar-coded manufacturing traveler is printed. This bar-coded traveler is used for deduct point and backflushing and to communicate to the equipment the specific item that is to be produced.

Result of full kanban implementation. For North Star the results of the full implementation are significant. Within two years they were able to

- Eliminate hard copy purchase orders
- Eliminate the need for buy cards
- Eliminate the stockroom
- Eliminate the need to farm out board assemblies
- Eliminate the need to phone in the orders to the suppliers
- Reduce phone and mailing costs
- Reduce material handling costs
- Significantly lower supplier lead times from weeks to days
- Reduce inventory by 65% while totally eliminating the need for shortage meetings
- Reduce the customer lead times by 90%
- Elevate customer on-time delivery from 75% to 99%

North Star's new automated kanban system has played a major role in making this company highly competitive.

North Star became extremely successful by applying a number of methodologies explained in this book, and thus it provides an overall good example. The only major technique they did not employ was the broadcast methodology, because it did not apply to their facility. The company described below, however, was highly successful in the application of the broadcast methodology, because the suppliers for their most expensive components were within a 75-mile radius of the facility.

PRECISION TAPE BACKUP

A tape backup manufacturer, let's call them Precision Tape Backup, was constantly trying to keep up with customer demand. The difficulty was that they needed to ship their products immediately after the customer placed an order; otherwise, they risked losing the order. Precision Tape Backup was primarily interested in significantly improving their internal quality levels, improving customer on-time delivery, and reducing obsolescence.

Product profile. Precision Tape Backup offers numerous standard models that compete in a highly competitive market. All the components were procured from the supplier base, and the final product was assembled and tested in-house. The bills of material were four levels deep. For Precision Tape Backup to remain competitive, it was vital to have high quality, immediate delivery, and low costs. A major concern in this business was the high obsolescence due to frequent model changes.

Component profile. The company had more than 1,000 active part numbers. The suppliers of the most expensive part numbers were located within a 75-mile radius of Precision Tape Backup's manufacturing facility. Here, 5% of the part numbers represented 90% of the dollars. These items consisted of tape drives, computer interface cards, power supplies, and packaging. Precision Tape Backup used the MRPII package to procure all their components. Their inventory turn ratio was around four turns, and the customer on-time delivery was 80%.

Precision Tape Backup manufacturing methodology. The Precision Tape Backup manufacturing plant was laid out in a traditional manner and everything was funneled through the stockroom. They ran the product in batches to minimize kit pulls and pulled the kits a week in advance to expedite any part shortages. They had a high-volume operation that experienced a high internal rejection rate. This meant that they needed technicians to analyze and troubleshoot each rejected unit. It was an expensive procedure that generated a consistently large quantity of units waiting to be analyzed and repaired.

Action taken to implement automated kanban. One of the first things Precision Tape Backup did was to construct work cells by product family. This eliminated the stockroom. By placing the components at the point of use, it also enabled a one-piece flow rather than building in batches. They reduced manufacturing lead times from eight days to two days.

There were other areas of improvement and preparation for implementing automated kanban. For instance, it was important for Precision Tape Backup to have better forecasting. Before kanban, marketing generated a final product forecast expressed in dollars that was very inaccurate. It was also difficult to convert dollars into the number of units, since prices were fluctuating by as much as 35%. This system was changed to using the historical database of the MRPII system, which kept track of past sales for a final product number by day and quantity. This was now used in predicting fairly accurate future sales. By programming a routine, the production control manager was able to

- Enter into the computer the number of *days of supply* he wanted to carry on the shelf for each model
- Tell the routine how far back to go into history to determine the *average sell rate per day* of each model
- Utilize a "times factor" to increase (that is, 1.05) or decrease (that is, 0.95) the calculated average sales rate per day, by model, based upon current information

The computer routine determined the average sell rate per day and automatically multiplied it by the days of supply for each model to be carried on the shelf. The computed number became the kanban lot size of the final product.

Determining the days of supply to carry on the shelf was very important because, by employing the kanban broadcast methodology, they were able to avoid overstocking the most expensive components. The days of supply to carry on-hand of finished goods were determined by the production control manager by taking the following into consideration:

- Longest supplier replenishment lead time of expensive components (which were not carried on hand) for a particular model
- Manufacturing lead time of the final product
- Safety stock for the final product

If, for example, the longest supplier replenishment lead time of the expensive components for final product model 34WRB is three days (one-day download frequency, two-day supplier lead time), the manufacturing lead time is two days, and the safety stock is one day, the production control manager would arrive at a six-day supply for final product model 34WRB. This information is then placed into the AFT system for that particular model. If the average sales rate per day was 100, the AFT system calculates a kanban lot size of 600 units (six-day supply times 100 average sales rate per day). Once a customer order is booked, the AFT system immediately allocates it against the finished-goods on-hand inventory. When the total of inventory on-hand and on-order drops below the 600 units, the single-container discrete option that is employed determines the quantity that falls below 600 units, which in this example is 75 units.

The AFT system then automatically creates purchase orders for 75 pieces (one per example) of each coded (expensive item) part number that goes into final product model 34WRB, and downloads the requirements to the supplier base. The AFT system then triggers a 75-unit requirement for final product 34WRB at the cell responsible for replenishment on the manufacturing queue screen. At the end of the third day (one-day download frequency + two-day longest supplier lead time), the AFT system automatically performs a parts availability simulation. If all the parts are available, it will show on the manufacturing queue screen at the cell responsible for replenishment as "OK," thus permitting the operator to print the manufacturing bar-coded travelers. As each manufacturing bar-coded traveler for the 75 pieces is printed, it subtracts from the 75 pieces required. This number reflects the remaining quantity to build. If there are shortages in the simulation, it will show these shortages in the queue screen and generate a shortage report.

Another improvement Precision Tape Backup implemented was designing the work cell so that the operator could assemble, test, and package for shipment. Now the operator can use the bar-coded manufacturing traveler to initiate the proper test on the testing equipment and for backflushing. If the unit fails the test, the operator is in a position to open it up, check the assembly work, make corrections, and retest. This process eliminated 75% of the defective units that were being routed to the technicians for analysis and repair.

Results Achieved

- The inventory turn ratio went from 4 turns to 17.
- Because of the zero inventory on high-dollar items, the frequent model changes in this business no longer generated high obsolescence.
- Customer on-time delivery went from 80% to 99%.
- A one-piece flow was achieved, which significantly improved customer response time.
- Rework by the technicians was reduced by 75%.

The single-, dual-, triple-, or multiple-kanban option should not be applied to an environment that has frequent model changes or engineering changes. The kanban broadcast methodology as applied to Precision Tape Backup was a perfect fit, because it attacked one of the worst wastes of all—obsolescence.

Although the AFT system is fully automated, certain aspects of it can and should remain manual if that makes sense in a particular situation. This scenario is demonstrated in the next example.

MEDICAL MONITORING

A medical monitoring equipment manufacturer in North America, which we will simply call Medical Monitoring, had high inventory levels, long internal and external lead times, and a customer on-time delivery of 84%. Their bookings were very linear, but they built in batches due to the non-value-added activities of kitting. The company wanted to improve customer on-time delivery, reduce manufacturing lead time, make shipments more linear, reduce inventory, and lower costs.

Company profile. Medical Monitoring offers 45 standard models that encompass 2,500 active part numbers. There is a high degree of commonality for the products' assemblies, subassemblies, and components. The types of assemblies include harness, cables, board assemblies, and mechanical assemblies. Before implementing automated kanban, the bills of material were four levels deep. The lead time quoted to the customer was six weeks, which represented the manufacturing lead time. Although the bookings were linear, 50 to 60% of the shipments occurred the last week of the month.

Medical Monitoring manufacturing methodology. The layout of the plant was traditional, with everything funneled through the stockroom. All Medical Monitoring products were built in batches. Their floor space was cramped, aggravated by the room needed for the batch process. They had an MRPII package that included MRP and order-point capability. They used the MRP module. Their inventory turn ratio equated to two turns. Shortages occurred, but infrequently.

Action taken to implement automated kanban. Medical Monitoring constructed work cells with the material located at the point of use, allowing them to engage in backflushing that eliminated the stockroom. This also enabled the floor to build to a quantity of one, since they no longer had to kit. Now they could produce a product within five days, counting a 72-hour (test) burn-in.

They also programmed a simplified kanban calculation routine to calculate the final product kanban lot size. It was programmed to pull up the bookings that had occurred for each model, going back three individual months, with the respective average daily demand for each model by month. The report includes current customer orders by model, and quantity of final product on the shelf. The operations manager inputs into AFT the anticipated daily demand for each product. The AFT system then multiplies the input average daily demand by the replenishment lead time and safety stock, which becomes the kanban lot size for the final product. Once the kanban lot size is solidified, the operations manager adds and subtracts the number of manufacturing travelers manually (the manufacturing travelers are premade and filed in a cabinet). Each unit that is built has a manufacturing traveler sitting with it on the finished-goods shelf. When a unit is pulled for shipment, the manufacturing traveler goes to the cell responsible for replenishment to initiate the build. As final product is built, it is kept track of and backflushed at the end of the day.

Medical Monitoring also took their parts procurement off the MRP system and placed it on the order point system. They took this step after solidifying yearly contracts with their suppliers, resulting in an overall 8% reduction in cost. Yearly contracts are usually preferable to negotiating pricing for small quantities of the same item repeatedly throughout the year. The suppliers also agreed to carry the lead-time quantity on the shelf, and the lead times in the computer were adjusted downward accordingly. The AFT system then took the average daily demand that was input for each final product and exploded it on MRP (on-hand and on-order were omitted from this explosion) to ascertain the average daily demand for each assembly, subassembly, and component. Next, AFT applied the average daily demand for each item times the replenishment lead time, plus safety stock, to equal the kanban lot size. The kanban lot size was then automatically loaded in the order point field. When the total of on-hand plus on-order falls below the kanban lot size, a purchase order is automatically created and downloaded to the supplier (single container, full application). For the make items the order point report was used to initiate action (single container, discrete application). This report was sorted by work cell. When the build is made it is logged onto the reorder point report. At the end of the day the reorder reports are turned in where they were backflushed at one computer terminal.

Results Achieved

- Customer on-time delivery went from 84% to 98%.
- Manufacturing lead time went from six weeks to five days.
- Average supplier lead time went from six weeks to four days.
- Cost of buy-components was reduced by 8%.
- Linear build reduced end-of-the-month overtime expenses.
- Linear shipments made the cash flow linear.
- Inventory levels were reduced by 54%.
- The majority of the replenishment systems' non-value-added activities were reduced.

The key to the design of this system is that it is for an extremely small facility. It has only six work cells with a short distance between them. It does not require computer terminals at each work cell; therefore, the finished-goods traveler is handled manually and the order point report is used for assemblies and subassemblies. The demand patterns in this environment are very linear and there is no lot-sizing of assemblies or subassemblies to consider when calculating kanban lot sizes because (1) the final assembly is a single-container discrete option, and (2) the assemblies and subassemblies have the same manufacturing replenishment lead times (one day) with no minimums or multiples and use a single-container discrete option. This simplified version of triggering and backflushing of make-items works very well for Medical Monitoring.

CONCLUSION

The AFT system is a competitive weapon that can yield substantial gains with minimal cost. It begins where just-in-time and manual kanban leave off. Without question, it is the next frontier in eliminating non-value-added activities and providing an agility that surpasses your competitors in responding to customer needs at a lower cost. At present, companies considered world class are still using a manual kanban system loaded with non-value-added activities. The majority of companies in North America still utilize an MRPII package that is also loaded with non-value-added activities coupled with an extremely poor execution methodology. You have a golden opportunity that is not going to stay open forever. It is better to make this a competitive weapon owned and operated by your company as opposed to waiting for your competitor to use it against your company.

I hope that this book has made you aware of the non-value-added activities that are associated with the current replenishment systems and how they impact your response capabilities and inflate the cost of your product. You now know the key concepts of the AFT system, including supplier contracts, kanban lot-size formulas, simulation methodologies, flexible work-cell staffing formulas, download methodology, execution methodologies, and perpetuation and implementation considerations. It is now up to you to design, implement, and perpetuate your own AFT system. I wish you well in your endeavor.

about the author

Mr. Louis is Director of Consulting with Productivity Consulting Group, a division of Productivity, Inc. He has extensive hands-on experience in transforming traditional manufacturers into world class manufacturers. His primary role with Productivity, Inc. is as Project Manager. In this capacity he assesses facilities, develops detailed implementation milestone charts, manages Productivity's resources in the conversion effort, and provides hands-on guidance on the shop floor with client personnel.

Prior to joining Productivity, Mr. Louis owned and operated his own consulting firm, specializing in WCM training and conversions.

In private industry, Mr. Louis held positions such as operations manager, production manager, materials manager, director of production control, purchasing manager, and inventory control manager with prominent national firms. In these capacities he has rectified major operational issues, fully implemented WCM techniques, and redesigned and implemented numerous MRPII packages. One of the WCM conversions in which he was heavily involved was named by *Industry Week* as one of America's 10 best companies.

Mr. Louis's methodology for WCM implementations has been published in periodicals such as *P&IM Review, ID Systems, Job Shop Tech-*

nology, Manufacturing Systems, and *Purchasing World.* He is the author of the book *How to Implement Kanban for American Industry,* published by Productivity Press, 1992.

He has taught courses at the University of California and California State University. He is also a frequent speaker for professional organizations such as the American Production Inventory Control Society.

Mr. Louis holds an MBA from the University of Phoenix, is Certified in Production and Inventory Management (CPIM) by the American Production and Inventory Control Society, and is a Certified Purchasing Manager (CPM) through the National Association of Purchasing Management.

Readers are encouraged to send any comments or questions to the author by e-mail: kuma2@ix.netcom.com

index

Books from Productivity Press

Productivity Press publishes books that empower individuals and companies to achieve excellence in quality, productivity, and the creative involvement of all employees. Through steadfast efforts to support the vision and strategy of continuous improvement, Productivity Press delivers today's leading-edge tools and techniques gathered directly from industrial leaders around the world. Call toll-free 1 (800) 394-6868 for our free catalog.

IMPLEMENTING TPM
The North American Experience
Charles J. Robinson and Andrew P. Ginder

The authors document an approach to TPM planning and deployment that modifies the Japan Institute of Plant Maintenance 12-step process to accommodate the experiences of North American plants. They include details and advice on specific deployment steps, OEE calculation methodology, and autonomous maintenance deployment. This book shows how to make TPM work in unionized plants and how to position TPM to support and complement other strategic manufacturing improvement initiatives. More than just an implementation guide, it's actually a testimonial of proven TPM success in North American companies through the adoption of "best in class" manufacturing practices.
ISBN 1-56327-087-0 / 224 pages / $45.00 / Order IMPTPM-B282

KAIZEN FOR QUICK CHANGEOVER
Going Beyond SMED
Kenichi Sekine and Keisuke Arai

Especially useful for manufacturing managers and engineers, this book describes exactly how to achieve faster changeover. Picking up where Shingo's SMED book left off, you'll learn how to streamline the process even further to reduce changeover time and optimize staffing at the same time.
ISBN 0-915299-38-0 / 315 pages / $75.00 / Order KAIZEN-B282

Productivity Press, Dept. BK, P.O. Box 13390, Portland, OR 97213-0390
Telephone: 1-800-394-6868   Fax: 1-800-394-6286

KANBAN AND JUST-IN-TIME AT TOYOTA
Management Begins at the Workplace
Japan Management Association
Translated by David J. Lu

Toyota's world-renowned success proves that with kanban, the Just-In-Time production system (JIT) makes most other manufacturing practices obsolete. This simple but powerful classic is based on seminars given by JIT creator Taiichi Ohno to introduce Toyota's own supplier companies to JIT. It shows how to implement the world's most efficient production system. A clear and complete introduction.
ISBN 0-915299-48-8 / 211 pages / $40.00 / Order KAN-B282

MANUFACTURING STRATEGY
How to Formulate and Implement a Winning Plan
John Miltenburg

This book offers a step-by-step method for creating a strategic manufacturing plan. The key tool is a multidimensional worksheet that links the competitive analysis to manufacturing outputs, the seven basic production systems, the levels of capability, and the levers for moving to a higher level. The author presents each element of the worksheet and shows you how to link them to create an integrated strategy and implementation plan. By identifying the appropriate production system for your business, you can determine what output you can expect from manufacturing, how to improve outputs, and how to change to more optimal production systems as your business needs change.
ISBN 1-56327-071-4 / 391 pages / $45.00 / Order MANST-B282

POKA-YOKE
Improving Product Quality by Preventing Defects
Nikkan Kogyo Shimbun Ltd. and Factory Magazine (ed.)

If your goal is 100 percent zero defects, here is the book for you—a completely illustrated guide to poka-yoke (mistake-proofing) for supervisors and shop-floor workers. Many poka-yoke devices come from line workers and are implemented with the help of engineering staff. The result is better product quality—and greater participation by workers in efforts to improve your processes, your products, and your company as a whole.
ISBN 0-915299-31-3 / 295 pages / $65.00 / Order IPOKA-B282

Productivity Press, Dept. BK, P.O. Box 13390, Portland, OR 97213-0390
Telephone: 1-800-394-6868   Fax: 1-800-394-6286

A REVOLUTION IN MANUFACTURING
The SMED System
Shigeo Shingo

The heart of JIT is quick changeover methods. Dr. Shingo, inventor of the Single-Minute Exchange of Die (SMED) system for Toyota, shows you how to reduce your changeovers by an average of 98 percent! By applying Shingo's techniques, you'll see rapid improvements (lead time reduced from weeks to days, lower inventory and warehousing costs) that will improve quality, productivity, and profits.
ISBN 0-915299-03-8 / 383 pages / $75.00 / Order SMED-B282
ISBN 0-915299-07-0 / 328 pages / $75.00 / Order ZQC-B282

TO ORDER: Write, phone, or fax Productivity Press, Dept. BK, P.O. Box 13390, Portland, OR 97213-0390, phone 1 (800) 394-6868, fax 1 (800) 394-6286. Outside the U.S. phone (503) 235-0600; fax (503) 235-0909
Send check or charge to your credit card (American Express, Visa, MasterCard accepted).

U.S. ORDERS: Add $5 shipping for first book, $2 each additional for UPS surface delivery. Add $5 for each AV program containing 1 or 2 tapes; add $15 for each AV program containing 3 or more tapes. We offer attractive quantity discounts for bulk purchases of individual or mixed titles; call for more information.

ORDER BY E-MAIL: Order 24 hours a day from anywhere in the world. Use either address:
To order: **info@productivityinc.com**
To view the online catalog and/or order: **http://www.productivityinc.com/**

QUANTITY DISCOUNTS: For information on quantity discounts, please contact our sales department.

INTERNATIONAL ORDERS: Write, phone, or fax for quote and indicate shipping method desired. For international callers, the telephone number is 503-235-0600 and the fax number is 503-235-0909. Prepayment in U.S. dollars must accompany your order (checks must be drawn on U.S. banks). When quote is returned with payment, your order will be shipped promptly by the method requested.

NOTE: Prices are in U.S. dollars and are subject to change without notice.

Productivity Press, Dept. BK, P.O. Box 13390, Portland, OR 97213-0390
Telephone: 1-800-394-6868   Fax: 1-800-394-6286

Productivity, Inc. Consulting, Training, Workshops, and Conferences

EDUCATION...IMPLEMENTATION...RESULTS

Productivity, Inc. is the leading American consulting, training, and publishing company focusing on delivering improvement technology to the global manufacturing industry.

Productivity, Inc. prides itself on delivering today's leading performance improvement tools and methodologies to enhance rapid, ongoing, measurable results. Whether you need assistance with long-term planning or focused, results-driven training, Productivity, Inc.'s world-class consultants can enhance your pursuit of competitive advantage. In concert with your management team, Productivity, Inc. will focus on implementing the principles of Value-Adding Management, Total Quality Management, Just-in-Time, and Total Productive Maintenance. Each approach is supported by Productivity's wide array of team-based tools: Standardization, One-Piece Flow, Hoshin Planning, Quick Changeover, Mistake-Proofing, Kanban, Problem Solving with CEDAC, Visual Workplace, Visual Office, Autonomous Maintenance, Overall Equipment Effectiveness, Design of Experiments, Quality Function Deployment, Ergonomics, and more! And, based on continuing research, Productivity, Inc. expands its offering every year.

Productivity, Inc.'s conferences provide an excellent opportunity to interact with the best of the best. Each year our national conferences bring together the leading practitioners of world-class, high-performance strategies. Our workshops, forums, plant tours, and master series are scheduled throughout the U.S. to provide the opportunity for continuous improvement in key areas of lean management and production.

Productivity, Inc. is known for significant improvement on the shop floor and the bottom line. Through years of repeat business, an expanding and loyal client base continues to recommend Productivity, Inc. to their colleagues. Contact Productivity, Inc. at 1-800-394-6868 to learn how we can tailor our services to fit your needs.